THE IN-DEMAND VIRTUAL ASSISTANT

THE 7-DAY GUIDE TO SMART STRATEGIES AND SOLUTIONS TO UNLOCK FINANCIAL FREEDOM AND CAREER FLEXIBILITY

ANNA MARIE RODRIGUES

To the Virtual Assistants, the unseen yet ever-present helpers who navigate the complexity of our digital lives with grace and efficiency—this book is dedicated to you.

To Clement, my rock, who transforms our home into a haven of creativity and productivity with his presence and work. Your dedication and love light up our world.

To Annamarie, my stepdaughter, who brings joy and vibrancy into our lives with her unique spirit and boundless energy.

To Robin, my eldest son, whose strength, wisdom, and kindness know no bounds. Your journey inspires us all.

To Ramon, my youngest son, a testament to the modern father who works from home and provides for his family, especially his son, Silas. Your dedication to balancing work and family life is nothing short of admirable.

To Silas, the beacon of our future, may you grow up in a world filled with love, knowledge, and compassion.

To Maila, my daughter-in-law, whose love and support created the foundation upon which our family stands strong. Your warmth and generosity fill our hearts with gratitude.

To Maximo and Gloria, my parents, who watch over us from heaven, your teachings and love guide us daily. You are our stars, shining brightly in the night sky.

To my sisters and their families, for the laughter, the tears, and everything in between. Your presence in my life is a gift I cherish deeply.

This book is a tribute to all of you, my family, and the virtual assistants we rely on daily. Together, you form the tapestry of my life, each thread interwoven with love, dedication, and the shared human experience. Thank you for being my inspiration, support, and reason.

With deepest gratitude and boundless love,

Anna Marie Rodrigues

TABLE OF CONTENTS

FOREWORD

As I write this foreword, I reflect on this journey that began in the quiet, unassuming corners of my home office, a place that has witnessed countless hours of aspiration, struggle, and eventual triumph. Long before the world was caught in the whirlwind of Covid-19, I was already navigating the waters of remote work. Driven to earn extra money, I endeavored to bring it to the next level. This wasn't for a lavish holiday or a new gadget but something far more pressing and personal—to improve my dad's healthcare situation.

The journey started almost serendipitously. While exploring ways to augment my income, I stumbled upon self-publishing. The ads made it seem so accessible and achievable. "Why not?" I thought. It was a decision that threw me headlong into the rollercoaster world of online entrepreneurship. Along the way, I experienced the full spectrum of highs and lows that come with trying to carve out a niche online. From online courses on publishing to creating content for my YouTube channel, each step was a leap into the unknown.

The decision to create a YouTube channel introduced me to the indispensable world of virtual assistants (VAs). Hiring VAs was a revelation; it opened my eyes to online business operations' complexities and potential. It wasn't all smooth sailing, of course. I had my share of hits and misses, learning the hard way what works and what doesn't in the virtual hiring arena. These experiences as a Virtual Assistant employer were enlightening, providing me with knowledge and insight that I felt compelled to share. Thus, the idea for this book was born.

Transitioning from a traditional 9 to 5 job to earning money online is a path fraught with challenges. It demands more than just a desire to change; it requires a strong motivation to persist and overcome the limiting beliefs that can hold one back. The most challenging milestones for me were releasing my first book and posting my first video on YouTube.

Initially, my dad was my driving force. Sadly, he passed away last December. Over time, he became my inspiration to continue, to push beyond my perceived limits. Despite the grief, I took solace in knowing that I was able to achieve what I set out to do—I published my first book in September and uploaded at least 10 videos before 2023 ended.

So, as you stand at the precipice of your journey into virtual assistance, I ask you, "What motivates you to step beyond your comfort zone?" Whatever your answer may be, grasp it firmly and let it guide you towards your goal. This book is not just a collection of advice and strategies; it is a testament to the resilience required to thrive in the online world. If I could navigate the tumultuous path of online entrepreneurship and come out stronger on the other side, so can you. Hold on to your motivation, and let it fuel your journey to becoming an in-demand Virtual Assistant.

Welcome to the first step of a rewarding journey. Let's dive in together.

INTRODUCTION

Are you feeling overwhelmed by the modern world's demands? Do you find yourself juggling an ever-expanding to-do list, striving to maintain work-life balance, or looking for a way to achieve financial security and personal empowerment? You're not alone. These difficulties have become commonplace in today's fast-paced digital world.

Another thing that has changed our world drastically is that conventional brick-and-mortar businesses are faced with the challenge of transitioning their business activities online to keep pace with industry trends. This shift is evident in the move from in-person to virtual client service. As a result, many companies are exploring collaborations with virtual assistants (VAs) to navigate this new terrain.

This book offers a comprehensive and actionable plan to become a highly effective VA in an ever-expanding digital marketplace. Inside, you will discover:

- A clear, realistic, and achievable career path
- Strategies to master the different VA-relevant skills
- Tips to enhance your competitiveness in the job market
- Guidance on building a recognizable personal brand
- Insights into achieving work-life balance that breaks frees from the traditional work structure
- Pathways to financial stability coupled with the flexibility of remote work
- A newfound sense of personal and professional empowerment

The digital era is opening many doors for all of us, and this book aims to unlock them for you.

CHAPTER ONE

THE RISE OF THE VIRTUAL ASSISTANT (VA)

The virtual assistance industry has seen remarkable global growth and expansion in recent years as more business leaders recognize and leverage the numerous benefits of working with professional VAs. As of this writing, the virtual assistance market is valued at approximately $3 billion and is projected to grow at an annual rate of 24.3% until 2030 (Grand View Research, 2018). Before delving into its future, let's explore how the VA role began to evolve within the industry.

THE EVOLUTION OF THE VIRTUAL ASSISTANCE INDUSTRY

The role of the VA has its roots in the 20th-century secretarial profession. It began in the early 1940s when Sir Isaac Pitman came up with the shorthand method, which marked the beginning of the secretarial services industry.

The very first school dedicated to secretarial services only catered to men, excluding women from the profession. However, the invention of the typewriter opened doors for women to penetrate the field. From then on, it only took a few years for women to dominate the field, almost completely displacing men from the sector. Technological advancements led to the typewriter being replaced by word processing systems, fax machines, and telephones. But when did the industry start to become virtual?

Commercialization of the internet began around 1994, facilitating easier global business trade and operations. It was around this time that the industry took its first step into the virtual realm, but it was only in 1996 that life coach Thomas Lenard and Anastasia Stacy Brice coined the term *"virtual assistance"*.

Stacy Briche, who worked as a secretary from home for her international clients, is considered one of the first VAs. The following year, the term gained traction and became a recognized profession under the company AssistU. Since then, the scope of secretarial tasks has expanded to include a wide range of services, such as project planning and management.

The Impact of the Gig Economy on VA Roles

The rise of the gig economy has had a significant impact on VA roles, leading to an increasing demand for professional VAs. Businesses of all sizes began to recognize the importance of VAs in scaling their operations. Utilizing VAs is cost-effective, offering companies the flexibility to scale up and down as needed without incurring additional costs such as insurance or committing to long-term contracts.

Additionally, the gig economy facilitated the rise of independent contractor setups, enabling VAs to work for multiple clients without conflicts of interest. During this period, VAs began to specialize in various roles beyond administrative tasks, taking on positions such as graphic designers and content writers.

Despite the negative impacts of the COVID-19 pandemic, it brought a much-needed shift to the virtual assistance industry. The pandemic completely transformed remote work, significantly increasing the demand for VAs capable of working remotely. As many businesses adapted to the remote work model, the demand for VAs grew, and the scope of the tasks they handled expanded accordingly.

TYPES OF VAS

There are many different types of VAs, typically divided into three distinct groups: general VAs, specialized VAs, and industry-specific VAs.

General VAs

Depending on the nature of business, some companies require specialized set of tasks aligned with their specific operations, while some need a broader spectrum of generalized services managed individually or as a team. General VAs are ideal for the latter. These VAs work alongside other employees to complete essential tasks and ensure everything is done correctly, alleviating the burden on others. Common tasks they handle include managing emails, booking travel, conducting market research, data entry, generating weekly reports, and answering customer inquiries, primarily focusing on administrative duties.

Specialized VAs

Specialized assistants can also perform general tasks, but they possess additional skills and expertise in specific fields required by certain types of businesses. Specialized VA services include website development and management, graphic design, social media management, human resources management, and order processing, to name a few. Due to their specialized knowledge, these VAs typically earn more than general VAs.

Industry-Specific VAs

Industry-specific VAs are the most specialized, and because of that, they often work exclusively within particular industries such as medical, legal, or real estate. These VAs usually charge higher fees in exchange for their highly specialized skill sets, backed by formal training and/or education.

WHY DO COMPANIES HIRE VAS?

Companies hire VAs for several reasons. VAs offer a cost-effective solution for businesses without office space, as they can work remotely. This setup also reduces operating costs, as VAs provide invaluable services to companies without the need for physical presence. By taking over various tasks such as note-taking or regular reporting, VAs help businesses save time, allowing other employees to focus on other things.

Another advantage is that VAs are only paid for the work they do unlike salaried employees, which can significantly reduce company costs. For companies that do not require full-time employees, hiring a VA is a practical solution. Additionally, VAs with specific skill sets can fill gaps that current employees cannot.

VAs also aid in business scalability. By prioritizing and delegating projects, business owners can efficiently scale their operations. The availability of VAs with diverse skill sets makes it easier for companies to find talent that meets their needs.

In addition, VAs allow businesses to gain access to a wide range of specialized skills they might not have in-house. The availability of

VAs in the market bearing diverse skill sets makes it easier for companies to hire talent according to their needs.

DEMAND TRAJECTORY FOR VAS

The COVID-19 pandemic significantly contributed to the exponential growth of the already booming VA market. The versatility of VA roles allows them to fit almost any industry, further driving demand. The increased use of the internet and social media also played a crucial role in this rise. Between July 2020 and July 2021, there was an increase of 257 million internet users and 520 million social media users (Tibon, 2020). By 2025, the VA market is projected to grow to $25.6 billion (MacKenzie, 2023), illustrating the profession's growing potential.

Specific cases, such as healthcare VAs, show significant market growth worldwide. For instance, in the US, the market was worth $502.7 million in 2022 (Markets, 2023). Forecasts indicate growth rates of 28.8% in China, 26.4% in Japan, and 24.5% in Canada from 2022 to 2030. The healthcare VA market in Germany is expected to grow by 18.6%.

Looking ahead, the VA market is likely to continue its global expansion despite challenges like worldwide conflicts and inflation. Businesses have shown resilience and adaptability during adversity, supporting the assumption that VA roles will continue to flourish.

INCOME POTENTIAL

The income potential for VAs varies widely based on industry, experience, and skill set. According to Payscale, VA salaries range from $22,000 to $60,000 per year, with hourly rates ranging from $10.75 to $27.46 and an average of around $17.84 (Payscale Team, n.d.).

Factors Affecting Income

1. **Experience**: Experienced VAs tend to earn more, as their expertise makes them stand out. Newcomers generally earn less until they gain more experience.
2. **Specialization**: Specialized VAs in high-demand fields can command higher salaries. For example, content marketing VAs make an average of $48,776 per year, e-commerce VAs around $32,700, graphic design VAs about $52,263, and lead generation VAs approximately $67,883 (We Are Indy Content Team, 2022).
3. **Location**: The average pay for VAs varies by location. In the US, states like Texas, Oregon, and Tennessee offer some of the highest average salaries, although entry-level pay may be below the national average. In cities like Seattle, Los Angeles, and New York, the discrepancy between the highest and lowest salaries is smaller, with higher entry-level pay. When comparing pay by country, Western locations generally offer higher wages than those in the East.
4. **Education and Training**: Higher education and specialized training can also increase a VA's income. Certain specialized tasks may require specific degrees or certifications.

Overall, VAs offer businesses a flexible, cost-effective solution while companies provide VAs with a dynamic and potentially lucrative career path.

SELF-ASSESSMENT

Let's take a quiz to see what type of VA role you might be better suited to perform. You must answer the following questions

honestly, and at the end of the quiz, tally up your scores to determine which type of VA role suits you best.

Questions

1. How would you describe your communication skills?

   A. Excellent. I love interacting with people (3 points)
   B. Good, but I prefer written communication (2 points)
   C. Decent, but I'd instead work behind the scenes (1 point)

2. What's your comfort level with technology?

   A. I am very comfortable, and I love exploring new tools
      (3 points)
   B. Comfortable enough to get the job done (2 points)
   C. I can manage, but it's not my strong suit (1 point)

3. How do you feel about multitasking?

   A. I thrive on it! (3 points)
   B. I can handle it, but I prefer to focus on one thing at
      a time (2 points)
   C. I'd rather avoid it if possible (1 point)

4. What's your approach to problem-solving?

   A. I'm proactive and love finding solutions (3 points)
   B. I can solve problems, but I prefer clear guidelines
      (2 points)
   C. I'd rather follow instructions than solve problems
      (1 point)

5. How do you feel about creative tasks like writing or design?

> A. I love them; creativity is my middle name! (3 points)
> B. I enjoy them but prefer a balance with other tasks
>   (2 points)
> C. Not my cup of tea (1 point)

Results

13–15 Points: The Customer Service Pro

You excel in communication and problem-solving, making you an ideal fit for customer service or client relations roles.

9–12 Points: The Tech-Savvy Organizer

You're comfortable with technology and good at multitasking. Roles involving project management or tech support would suit you well.

5–8 Points: The Specialized Skillmaster

You prefer focused tasks and may have specialized skills. Roles like data entry, content creation, or bookkeeping could be your forte.

* * *

In summary, the virtual assistance profession has evolved significantly over many decades, driven by technological advancements and large-scale global events such as the COVID-19 pandemic. The industry is expected to continue to continue its growth, as evidenced by past trends and future projections discussed in this chapter. A VA's average income varies widely based on factors such as specialization, experience, and location, with some entry-level VAs earning more in certain states and countries. If you decide to pursue this career, begin by identifying the VA role that best aligns with your skills and preferences. The quiz above can help you narrow down your options and make a more informed decision.

In the next chapter, we will discuss the essential skills needed to become a successful VA.

CHAPTER TWO

ESSENTIAL SKILLS FOR SUCCESS AS A VIRTUAL ASSISTANT

S uccess as a Virtual Assistant is largely dependent on one's possession of a particular set of skills. This chapter will delve into the essential competencies required for success in this field. It is often stated that skills are the currency of the 21st century, a sentiment that holds significant truth. In today's highly competitive environment, possessing a diverse skill set provides a substantial advantage over competitors. This is particularly pertinent given the considerable evolution of the global job market in recent years.

SOFT SKILLS

Soft skills are general traits not specific to any job, but they significantly enhance your performance. An example of a crucial soft skill is communication, both written and verbal. Clear and effective communication facilitates connections between individuals and, most importantly, prevents miscommunication. This is especially important for a VA who must be in constant communication with their bosses, coworkers, and clients. Active listening is vital aspect of effective communication, enabling the VA's ability to achieve client satisfaction by fully understanding the client's needs and expectations.

Time management skills are also essential. To succeed in this role, you must efficiently manage your time, as many tasks are time-consuming with strict deadlines dictated by business needs. The ability to identify and prioritize mission-critical tasks is vital for effective time management. Essentially, you need to know how to allocate your time, develop discipline, and stick to your timetable.

Time management encompasses other important skills, one of which is project management. This involves using productivity tools for each given project to manage your time better. Planning and scheduling are two more critical skills required of VAs that are often overlooked. These skills ensure process efficiency and ultimately lead to higher productivity.

TECHNICAL SKILLS

Technical skills are essential for specialized VA work. VAs are expected to be proficient with word processing software, which include data input and text formatting, rather than just fast typing. Additionally, they must be adept with productivity platforms and collaboration tools, as their services are primarily virtual. Proficiency in both MS Office and Google Workspace is crucial and often a requirement for any VA.

Some specific VA roles require additional technical skills, such as basic coding in HTML or CSS, as well as data analysis capabilities. These skills enable VAs to handle a broader range of tasks and provide more specialized support to their clients.

INDUSTRY-SPECIFIC SKILLS

One of the most sought-after industry-specific skills is Search Engine Optimization (SEO), particularly used in marketing. Understanding and selecting the best keywords can significantly impact a company's website. This involves knowing how to increase website ranking and optimizing the website organically, ultimately boosting website traffic and, consequently, the company's sales.

For those with medical backgrounds aiming to work as virtual healthcare assistants, proficiency in reviewing medical records for accuracy and scheduling appointments for patients or physicians is essential. These tasks require coordination with healthcare professionals, making medical training vital for understanding medical terminology. Effective communication is crucial for facilitating virtual interactions within the healthcare sector.

A legal VA is a skilled professional who provides remote assistance to legal practitioners and law firms. They must understand legal documents, since they are often the first to handle legal paperwork before it reaches the lawyer or the law firm. This initial review is essential, as is familiarity with legal jargon to effectively communicate with lawyers and other legal professionals.

CONTINUOUS LEARNING

To maintain your advantage over other VAs, you must constantly update your skills by continuous learning. As a VA, you need to keep yourself abreast of technological advancements. This ensures that your skills remain relevant and that you are kept informed about changes in your specific field. Advances in technology give rise to new tools being introduced in the market, and it is crucial for you be informed of these advancements and leverage new tools as they become available. This is vital to ensure that you are always ahead of, or at least at par with, increasing competition in your field.

Exploring Courses and Certifications

Facilitating continuous learning is essential for professional growth, and one effective way to achieve this is through courses and certifications. Enhancing your knowledge and skills can set your profile apart from other VAs, providing you with a competitive edge in the job market and enabling you to deliver better services to clients.

There are three main certifications for VAs that merit consideration. The first is the Certified Administrative Professional (CAP) certification, recognized globally by the International Association of Administrative Professionals (IAAP). Tailored for individuals aiming to demonstrate their proficiency in various administrative tasks, this certification signifies a high level of competence. While the exam requires effort, it covers crucial topics such as records management, organizational communication, office systems, and project management, significantly enhancing job prospects and opening up numerous career opportunities

Another valuable credential is the Certified Virtual Assistant (CVA) certification, specifically designed for VAs. Unlike the more general CAP, the CVA certification is more specialized and dependent on the chosen specialization. Candidates undergo training to demonstrate comprehensive understanding of the course material, making it highly sought after by clients seeking certified VAs.

Lastly, the Project Management Professional (PMP) certificate is renowned as the premier certification in project management. Offered by the Project Management Institute (PMI), obtaining this certification requires completion a specified number of project management hours, signifying expertise in the field.

While these certifications are widely recognized, there are numerous other courses available for specialization. Platforms like The SavvySystem, 90 Day VA, and Virtual Excellence Academy offer a plethora of courses catering to various areas of expertise. While these may not be as globally recognized as the aforementioned certifications, they are invaluable for honing specific skills and expertise tailored to individual career paths. It's crucial to explore these options and choose courses that best align with your career goals and aspirations.

NETWORKING

Networking is paramount in the virtual assistance industry, particularly for those just starting out. Building a professional network has become significantly easier with the advent of the internet. You can search for local groups and forums relevant to your professional interests and industry. Additionally, consider joining local communities where you can network in person, if that aligns with your preferences.

Leveraging Existing Connections

Despite being at the early stages of your VA career, it's important to leverage existing connections. You may believe you lack industry connections, but it's worth remembering that VAs operate in virtually every industry. Reach out to colleagues, former classmates, friends, and acquaintances. They may already be working in the industry or know someone who is, and could potentially be seeking VA services. Attend local and nationwide events, conferences, and seminars, even if they're not specifically VA-related. Opportunities to connect with potential clients or collaborators abound in diverse professional settings.

Using Online Platforms

Online platforms, particularly LinkedIn, are invaluable for networking in your professional life. Create a polished profile and connect with industry peers, while also joining relevant groups to expand your network.

Moreover, as a VA, you can offer valuable services to clients on LinkedIn to enhance their careers. Manage their LinkedIn company page, promote their business, and maintain regular updates. Expand their network by finding connections within the industry and engaging with their audience. Understanding LinkedIn's functionalities and leveraging them effectively is a crucial skill for any VA.

SELF-ASSESSMENT

Using the insights gained from this chapter, take the time to assess your VA skills, noting both your strengths and areas requiring improvement. This self-awareness will guide you in determining the type of VA role that best aligns with your abilities and aspirations.

As emphasized throughout this chapter, a diverse skill set can significantly impact your career as a VA. With numerous types of VAs and industries to choose from, the path you take is ultimately yours to decide. In the upcoming chapter, we'll explore tools and apps that can enhance your skills as a VA, increasing your chances of securing rewarding job opportunities.

CHAPTER THREE

TOOLS AND APPS OF THE TRADE FOR SAVVY VAS (PART 1)

T he right tools can make a five-hour job take five minutes. Much like with skills, a VA's success is also based on knowing the right tools and apps to use. In this chapter, we will be looking at getting familiar with essential tools for the many tasks you might come across as a VA.

COMMUNICATION TOOLS AND APPS

Effective tools are crucial for enhancing the efficiency and quality of your work. The tools highlighted in the subsequent paragraphs hold particular significance as they are widely utilized by VAs worldwide. Clients anticipate VAs to be proficient in using these tools, making them essential for delivering high-quality services.

Slack

Slack is a messaging platform or app where people within the same group can send messages, work together, and link to their tools. To set up on a desktop, first, you need to go to **https://slack.com/**

get-started#/createnew, sign up by entering your email, or use your Google or Apple account. Then, you must go back to your email and check the confirmation code. You enter the code and click "Create a Workspace." On an iOS or Android device, you first need to download the Slack app, add your email the same way you would on a desktop, confirm your email, and create a new workspace.

As previously mentioned, Slack offers messaging features, as well as the ability to share media or files, start voice or video calls, plan and manage projects, and support many tools that you can integrate with the app. It's an excellent tool when it comes to collaborating in or out of the office. It's very user-friendly, so you know exactly what you need to do even if it's the first time you're using it. It also gives you smooth integration, and it has over 170 bots and 2400 apps that you can integrate. It's also highly customizable with a variety of themes, channels, sidebars, etc. While Slack is a dedicated chat app, it's also an all-in-one chat app that allows you to integrate third-party tools, manage projects, and do great and smooth collaborative work. Besides that, it also offers great security against unauthorized access.

Slack's workspace members can invite new members into the workspace, however, only admins can make changes. It's quite easy to send an invitation: on a desktop, just click on the name of the workspace on the sidebar, click "Invite people to...", enter their email, and simply click "Send." On an iOS or Android device, it is equally simple; just go to the Home tab, tap on the three dots (which might be vertical or horizontal, depending on the device you have), then tap "Invite Members," enter their email, and send.

You can also customize member profiles, where you can, among other things, add time zones or job titles. Here, you just need to go and click on the workspace name, click on "Tools & Settings," and then click on "Workspace Settings." From there, you click on the menu and select "Profiles." You can then add people or data elements and simply follow the instructions. When you're done with your preferred customizations you can simply click "Publish Changes."

Setting Up Channels

One of the main features of Slack is its ability to create numerous channels, so all different topics of conversation are separate. There's no limit to the number of channels you want to create, so you can even divide teams into different channels. On a desktop, you can create a channel by clicking on the "+" button in the sidebar and then clicking on "Select a Channel." You can then give the new channel a name and choose if you want the channel to be public or private. On iOS and Android devices, you first must tap on the home menu at the bottom of the screen and tap on "+ Add Channel," then tap on "Create Channel" on iOS devices or tap on the "+" sign for Android devices. You can then enter a channel name, add a description, and choose if you want a public or private channel.

Notifying Team Members

There are a few ways to notify individuals or groups of individuals on Slack, but the main ones are @everyone and @channel. You can only use @everyone in the general channel, where every member of the Slack workspace is automatically invited. You can use this to give general information. For instance, you can use @channel to notify everyone who belongs to that specific channel. You can use this to update your team.

There's another notification that might be useful. This is @here, and you can notify people who are actively working in any channel that you are a member of. This is a great way to get the attention of people working on the same things as you and not notify those who are not available at the time. For instance, you can use this if you need to schedule an event or have a question that needs a quick answer.

Pinning Messages

You can pin messages on any channel or send a direct message. This functionality is useful if you want important messages to be seen or if you want to add bookmarks. This way, every single channel member can see or have access to them.

You can pin a message from a desktop by hovering over the message that you want to pin, then clicking on the three dots and clicking on "Pin to channel." You can do the same thing if you want to pin a message to a direct message. To remove it, you first need to open the direct message or the channel and click on the pinned message. If you hover your mouse over the message, you can click on the "X" icon that appears. Then you just confirm that you want to unpin the message. You must tap and hold the message you want to pin for mobile devices. You can do the same thing to unpin any message.

When it comes to bookmarks, from your desktop, you need to open the direct message or the channel, click on the "+" icon, and then add a bookmark. You can copy and paste a link and simply click "Add." To delete a bookmark, go to the direct message or desktop, right-click on the bookmark, and select delete (or edit if you want to edit the bookmark). Then, all you have to do is save the changes or confirm you want to delete the bookmark.

Integrations

Let's now discuss one of Slack's best features: integration, and how it all works to enhance your skills.

Automating Tasks

The automatic tasks on Slack are linked to a workflow, and they all start with a trigger. Some triggers start a workflow automatically, such as scheduling a date and time. Others might start when an individual performs an action. The trigger starts automatically and follows the workflow when this action is done. For instance, you can send these workflows in messages or bookmark them in channels.

Tracking Progress

There are many ways to track progress on Slack. As a VA, you should know how important it is to track projects. A failed project can be costly to you, the team, and the company. Therefore, by tracking projects, you can stay on schedule, within the budget, or maximize resources. Now, how exactly can you track the progress of projects? One way is through team meetings. You can simply schedule these meetings when you want, whether it be weekly, monthly, in person, or via video conference. You can use the chat to update tasks or identify any issues you or your team are having. So, when you must meet virtually, Slack allows you to integrate Microsoft Teams or Zoom, so you don't have to open different apps when joining meetings. If you need to do one-on-ones but you're not in the same place, then Slack supports private messaging and one-on-one video calling through the built-in messaging chat.

Another way you can track progress is through timesheets, so you know how long members of your team spend on different tasks. Slack allows integration with timesheet software such as Quidlo Timesheets or TrackingTime, so you can track and share the time people spend on each task.

You can also add task updates, and Slack allows you to integrate task management tools such as Flow, Wrike, or Asana so you can post different tasks and updates on projects while still on the platform. The same goes for status reports. Slack supports collaborative file sharing and can integrate cloud storage like Dropbox, Google Drive, or OneDrive.

Another great feature is the ability to create a poll. You can choose between two apps already integrated into Slack: Polly or Simple Poll. To start a poll, click "Compose" to begin a message. Then, add the voting options and send your message.

Zoom

Zoom is a software and app that allows one-on-one or group video calls where you can have meetings, chat with your team, and do many other things.

Setting Up

You can download Zoom on your desktop or on an iOS or Android device. All you have to do is go to Zoom's website if you are using a desktop or go to the App Store (on iOS) or Google Store (on Android) for use on a mobile device. The installation is automatic on mobile devices. However, on desktops, there are a few steps, albeit uncomplicated. Depending on the type of computer you have, you can choose to download the Zoom desktop client for Windows, macOS, or Linux. You can also download many different plugins from the same website if you wish to do so. After you've downloaded the version for the desktop you wish to use, you can double-click on the Zoom icon, and it starts the installation.

Important Features

Zoom's main feature is meetings, plus other different options that can enhance your experience such as participant engagement features. To create and use a continuous meeting chat that allows you to meet any meeting participants before, during, or after a meeting, you can create a dedicated group chat. You can also create polls in meetings while on the video call, as well as quizzes.

Another great feature is meeting breakouts, where you can split Zoom calls into 100 sessions. This is ideal if many different teams are working on different parts of a single project. If you are a host or a co-host, you can jump between sessions any time you'd like.

Creating schedules for meetings is also an essential feature of Zoom, and you can do this in multiple ways. You have full control over the scheduled meetings if you are the host. There are also other features, such as livestream meetings or different languages.

Microsoft Teams

Microsoft Teams is, in many ways, like Zoom. Here, you can chat with anyone or with a group to talk about a project.

Getting Started

You can create a team and different channels to gather different individuals for different projects and work in a place where you can communicate and share files.

There's the calendar feature that is synced to Microsoft Outlook and the ability to connect with the team before, during, or after a meeting. It also has many different integrations and is very easy to customize.

How to Obtain, Install, and Set Up

You can go to the Microsoft Teams download page on your desktop and click Download Teams. This will prompt you to log in to your Microsoft account, and if you don't have one, you must sign up. After you've done that, the download will start automatically. Then, all you have to do is install it and click on the message, "Let's do this!"

Important Functions and Features

Microsoft Teams has many different features that will make your life much easier including one-on-one chat messaging and group chat. There is also the mentions feature, much like you do in Slack, such as using "@" before the person's name, contact search, conversation search, assistant bots, or even message threads, among many other features.

File Sharing and Collaboration

Like Slack, Teams allows you to share files and collaborate in chat groups. This application also uses cloud file sharing, so you can always access your files and know they are secure. You can share virtually any type of file, from Word to PDF to spreadsheet, and it's very intuitive.

PROJECT MANAGEMENT TOOLS AND APPS

In this section, we will discuss project management tools and apps that helps VAs in effectively managing workloads, supporting coordination and communication, and in increasing productivity. Let's look at some of the most common ones currently available:

Asana

Asana is an excellent project management tool that allows teams to collaborate, plan, and perform different tasks. Setting up an account is easy; you can simply go to Asana's website and sign up. Once you've confirmed your email, you will go through a short wizard interface where you will be required to answer some questions, like what your role is and other general questions, so the software customizes Asana for you.

Once you are on the main screen to start organizing projects and tasks, you must first start a blank project by going to the left-hand menu and choosing "Create a Project." While you can choose a blank project, you can also choose other options, such as using a template or importing a spreadsheet. Once that is done, you can start setting up your project by giving it a name and filling in other details that appear in the same window. Then, you can go to projects by clicking on "Go to Project," which will open a new project page, and you can start adding different tasks. You can choose from more options, but this is the most basic. There are also plenty of tutorials that you can choose from to deepen your knowledge of the software.

Another feature that may be worthy to highlight is the ability to set deadlines for projects. Timelines are essential especially when planning for your project even before it starts. In Asana you can create tasks in list or board view and then go to timelines to begin mapping out deadlines. This can be as simple as dragging unscheduled tasks onto the timeline.

Trello

Trello is an incomparable visual tool that allows you and your team to manage any type of project. It has all the basic functionalities you'd expect, such as adding files, checklists, automation, and much more.

Trello works on many devices, such as your laptop or desktop, mobile device, and browser. Computer users simply have to go to the Trello website and sign up. You can then work directly in your browser or download the desktop version. Mobile device users simply have to download the Trello app from the download store (either the iOS or Android store). The installation is automatic, and you just need to sign up to get started.

Important Features

Trello is a great application that can increase your productivity. Utilizing the app can help you manage tasks with ease. Trello uses cards where you can gather information that you and your team need to have everything organized in one place. You can also leave comments, assign members to perform different tasks, add dates, etc. This is a great way to keep your team accountable simply by adding members to cards on the different projects that you have going on. The same goes for dates, such as due dates. As with most software, you can attach files to cards and projects, and it's as simple as dragging and dropping files onto the different cards. Checklists are also an essential part of this software and often of your job. You can simply break down bigger tasks into smaller ones and check them off the list when they are done.

Using Boards and Cards

There are two important things to take into consideration when you start using Trello: boards and cards, since these are vital parts of the software. Boards are a place where you can track different projects and get information about them. Not only that, but you can also create boards to track teams and workflows. It's a great way to keep everything organized on one board. On the boards, you can also have lists of where you keep your cards. These often have specific tasks or information, and you can organize them in phases of progress as your project moves forward. These lists are often used to generate your workflow, and the cards can be dragged and dropped as you see fit across these lists. Because there's no limit to lists and cards, you can track large projects with ease.

In Trello, cards are the smallest unit of your board and can be used to show information, tasks, or ideas. For instance, a card can represent something you need to do, such as a task or information that needs to be remembered. All you have to do when on a board is click "Add a card," and a card will be created. You can customize these cards the way you like them with a simple click.

Adding Members

It's easy to add members to a board when using Trello. First, go to the board to which you'd like to add members and click "Share" from the menu. Then, you can look for the members you want to add by email or name and invite them. If you are the board's admin, you don't need any permission, but if you're not, only the admin can add new members.

You can also check the "Suggested Users" list Trello creates, which is a list based on people that you've worked with in the past. Even if you're not using Trello or have access to the board yet, you can still add them by sending an invitation when opening Trello and simply clicking on "Send invitation."

You can also add non-members as a boarding guest who can see the board but is not a member.

Jira

Jira is another project management tool that allows you and your team to track, manage, and organize your projects. Getting started with Jira is easy. The first thing to do is to choose your installation method. The official website offers many different choices, such as installing the trial if you just want to try it out, installing the software using an installer, or even installing it from a zip or archive file. In all these cases, you just must select your operating system, whether it is Windows, Linux, or macOS.

Once you've installed the software, you just must follow a few steps to get it to work. The first step is to create a project, which you can only do once you've signed up on Jira's website. Then, once you're done with it, you just need to open the software and click "Projects," following "Create project." Here, you will have the option to choose a template. There are many you can choose from, and each is designed for a specific functionality. If you and your team work from a backlog, you can plan and estimate work using sprints. You can also monitor work in a continuous workflow or even track any bugs that might occur.

Important Features

Now, let's move on to the features that make Jira an excellent project management software. The software is based on boards, and here you can choose between two functionalities within the boards: Scrum and Kanban. You can also plan and track your work with timelines to make sure everyone is in sync. One of the best features of Jira is its reports. In addition, Jira allows for over 3000 apps and integrations, so you can maximize your performance.

Agile Workflows

One of the most predominant features of Jira is its agile workflow. This is essentially a series of stages that teams can use to create an application. Here, you will find three main components: status, transition, and resolution. The status simply tells you the status of the project, such as in progress or in review, among others. Transition is moving an issue or task from one status to another. Resolution is when the task is complete, and you can close it.

Reporting

Jira's reporting tool is, without a doubt, one of the best in the market. It's highly detailed, which allows you to deliver value to your customers much faster with its real-time insights. These insights allow you and your team to make data-driven decisions.

DOCUMENTS MANAGEMENT TOOLS AND APPS

A significant aspect of the VA role involves organizing documents, which can often feel overwhelming. Document management tools significantly ease this task, making it more manageable. Let's explore some of these tools and apps:

Google Drive

Google Drive is a personal cloud storage service that also allows you to share files with others. It's free to use up to 15 gigabytes of storage, which includes Google Photos and Gmail.

Obtaining Google Drive

You don't have to install Google Drive on your desktop; you can simply go to their website and register. There you will find "My Drive," where you can create, upload, or sync files. You can create many documents and files, such as Google Docs, Sheets, Forms, or Slides. You can upload, create, and work on Office files as mentioned.

Main Features

Google Drive is a fantastic tool with plenty of great features that allow you to perform your job more efficiently. Looking at team collaboration, Google Drive allows for the ability to collaborate with other people in real time on many documents, such as documents or sheets. Up to 50 different people can work on a single document wherever they are if they have access to the internet. Best of all, everyone can see the changes you or someone else made, and you can simply go back to check the unaltered versions of the same document. This feature is called "Revision history" and allows you to go back to see any changes. So, even if someone deletes something by accident, it's never truly lost.

Also, there's another feature called "Suggestion mode," where anyone can suggest a change without changing it first. If you are the document's admin, you can set it to "Comments only." Others can only comment without changing the document itself. There's even a chat function on any document where you can share ideas with others who are using the same document.

Another great feature of Google Drive is the ability to share documents and folders with people outside of your team and even outside your organization. You can share it with up to 200 different emails, whether for commenting, suggesting, or just viewing. If you are the admin, you can invite people and give them different permissions.

Google Drive allows for advanced search features, which come in handy if you use the platform and have many different files (especially if you are a VA). You can even search within documents or files and look for specific words. Uploading files from outside the drive couldn't get any easier. All you have to do is drag and drop. Of course, you can use the more traditional way to search for documents outside by typing the document on your computer.

With mobile applications (also free), you can save any image using the camera. When you take a picture, the driver will save it to Google Drive immediately. Google Drive also has Optical Character Recognition (OCR), which allows you to turn any characters and words in a picture into a PDF or Doc file.

If you are like most VAs, you will have tons of different files and documents, but some are more important than others. This is where the "Starred" functionality comes in handy, where they are placed in a special folder on the sidebar where you can quickly find them. There's also the "recent" folder, where you can access other folders and documents you've used recently.

Google Drive allows you to convert other files into Google Drive-readable and editable files automatically. For instance, if you have a Word file, you can upload it to Google Drive and automatically convert it into a Doc file, where you can edit it. To activate this feature, you just need to go to "Settings", "General," and tick "Convert Uploads." You can also view any type of file, such as PDFs, Word files, or even the most common image files, such as JPGs and PNGs.

There are also many add-ons, which are additional functionalities that you can add to your Google Drive and documents.

Dropbox

Dropbox is like Google Drive but without the built-in word processor, slides, or spreadsheets. It's a cloud storage service where you can sync content, share files and folders, and collaborate with many other people wherever you are if you have an internet connection.

To download and install Dropbox on your desktop, simply go to the website and choose the right operating system. Alternatively, there's also a mobile app, so you can have Dropbox on the go.

Features

One of Dropbox's best features is its ability to organize. You can add any traditional files or cloud content to one place, store and access any files anywhere, and even back up important files and folders. You can also edit and create using Microsoft Office software like Word and switch between apps.

The sync functionality is also good. This allows you to keep files and other documents accessible. Not only that, but you can also use different apps, such as Zoom or Slack, without leaving Dropbox. You can activate notifications, and when there's an update on the progress, you will know. Besides Slack and Zoom, Dropbox has many other integrations that can help you become more efficient.

Dropbox is also very secure. People whom you have given permission to are the only ones with access to the files, but there are other features that you can implement, such as expiring links, passwords, or even download permissions. Like Google Drive, you can protect any folders or files from unwanted edits or even viruses, and you can recover anything on your account for up to 30 days before they are eliminated.

OneDrive

OneDrive is dedicated to Microsoft Cloud storage and has functions similar to Google Drive or Dropbox. It is completely integrated with Microsoft Office and allows you to connect with Outlook for emails and even your Xbox (not that this will help you become more productive).

It's easy to install. All you need to do is go to the official website, click on download, check the correct version for your desktop, and open it. You also need to sign in or create an account if you don't have one yet.

Any of the apps or software we've discussed here can really improve your job efficiency. Now, you don't have to use them all, and it's important that you pick the ones that work best for you. For example, you don't need three different drives; usually, one is enough, but using the one suited to your work can do wonders for how you collaborate with your team.

INVENTORY STEPS

Slack

Setting up

Desktop

- Visit Slack's website.
- Sign up with your email or use a Google or Apple account.
- Check your email for a confirmation code.
- Enter the code and click "Create a workspace."
- **iOS/Android**
- Download the Slack app.
- Add an email, confirm, and create a new workspace.

Inviting Members

Desktop

- Click on the workspace name.
- Select "Invite people to..."
- Enter your email and click "Send."
- **iOS/Android**
- Go to the Home tab.
- Tap three dots, then "Invite members."
- Enter your email and send it.

Customizing Member Profiles

- Click on the Workspace name.
- Navigate to "Tools & Settings" and then "Workspace Settings."
- Click on "Profiles" in the menu.
- Add details and click "Publish changes."

Setting Up Channels

- **Desktop**
- Click "+" in the sidebar.
- Click "Select a channel," name it, and choose public or private.
- **iOS/Android**
- Tap the home menu, then click "+ add channel."
- Enter a name, add a description, and choose public or private.

Notifying Team Members

- Use @everyone (general channel), @channel (specific channel), or @here (active members).

Pinning Messages

- **Desktop**
- Hover over the message, click three dots, and choose "Pin to channel."
- To remove, click the pinned message, hover, and click "X."
- **Mobile**
- Tap and hold the message to pin or unpin.

Integrations

- Explore and integrate third-party tools.

Automating Tasks

- Set up workflows with triggers for task automation.

Tracking Progress

- Use channels, timesheets, task updates, and status reports.

Zoom

Setting up Zoom

- Download from Zoom's website, App Store, or Google Store.
- Install and open.

Important Features

- Explore participant engagement, continuous meeting chat, polls, quizzes, meeting breakouts, and scheduling.

Microsoft Teams

Getting Started

- Download from the Microsoft Teams page.

Important Functions and Features

- Explore one-on-one chat, group chat, mentions, contact search, conversation search, assistant bots, and message threads.

Asana

Getting Started

- Sign up on Asana's website.
- Complete the setup wizard.

Setting Up Projects

- Create a project, choose Options (template, import, etc.), and add details.

Setting Deadlines

- Use timelines to map out project deadlines.

Trello

Getting Started

- Sign up on Trello's website.
- Choose a browser or download a desktop or mobile app.

Using Boards and Cards

- Understand boards for project tracking and lists for workflow.
- Create cards for tasks and customize them.

Adding Members

- Go to the board, click "Share," and invite members by email or name.

Jira

Getting Started

- Choose the installation method on Jira's website.

Important Features

- Explore Scrum and Kanban boards, Agile workflows, timelines, and reporting.

Google Drive

Obtaining Google Drive

- Access Google Drive's website.
- Create/upload/sync files in "My Drive."

Main Features

- Collaborate in real-time, use revision history, suggestion mode, and share files and folders.
- Utilize advanced search, mobile applications, and file conversion.

Dropbox

Getting Started

- Download from Dropbox's website.
- Install and sign in.

Features

- Organize files, sync content, edit or create using Microsoft Office, and utilize sync functionality.
- Ensure security with permissions, expiring links, passwords, and download restrictions.

OneDrive

Getting Started

- Download from OneDrive's website.
- Install and sign in.

Features

- Integrated with Microsoft Office, Outlook, and Xbox.
- Explore file sharing and collaboration.

CHAPTER FOUR

TOOLS AND APPS OF THE TRADE FOR SAVVY VAS (PART 2)

I n this chapter, we will delve deeper into additional tools and apps designed to enhance your effectiveness as a VA. Specifically, we'll explore various types of time management and financial tools that serve to bolster productivity, streamline operations, and facilitate effective financial management.

TIME MANAGEMENT TOOLS AND APPS

We've emphasized the critical importance of time management for VAs. With numerous clients, deadlines, tasks, and sometimes teams to handle, effective time management is essential for success.

These tools enable you to prioritize tasks, a fundamental skill in time management. VAs often begin their day by identifying high-priority tasks, and certain tools can be invaluable for this purpose. They organize tasks based on importance, priority, and urgency, recognizing that not all tasks require the same level of attention and focus.

Time management apps are particularly useful for setting clear goals and deadlines crucial for effective collaboration with clients. They ensure you remain updated on task progress and equipped to communicate effectively. Additionally, time blocking, a highly effective technique, involves allocating dedicated blocks of time for specific tasks. Many apps support this method, aiding in defining and adhering to these time blocks. Let's explore some of the top time management tools and apps available on the market.

Clockify

In basic terms, Clockify is a time tracker app as well as a timesheet that allows you to track your own hours working for different clients and across different projects.

Getting Started

There are free and paid versions of Clockify, and while the paid version has more features, the free version is an excellent one to begin with. The first thing you must do is create an account. To do this, you simply need to go to Clockify's website and sign up for free. All you need is your email address to create a password.

Then you must choose a plan. It is recommended to start with the free version, and it will be quite easy to upgrade should you find the application useful and would want to utilize the more advanced features. All you have to do is click "Upgrade" on the main page once you sign in. The paid versions are quite cheap, too, and come with different plans. For instance, the monthly billing (you can also choose annual billing, which is even cheaper) ranges between $3.99 and $11.99, depending on the plan you choose.

Once you have completed all of that, a workspace will automatically be created for you. If you need others for other projects, you can simply add more by clicking on "Manage." Keep in mind that each workspace is completely independent, so the data and teams will be separate.

In the profile settings, you can add your personal information and a picture if you'd like. You can also set different preferences, such as language or time zone. However, this doesn't mean all members in that workspace need to have the same language or time zone settings; they can choose their own.

Then, you can move on to the workspace setting where you need to set up your data related to time-tracking. This depends on how you want it to be displayed and even on the type of business you have. The categorizing time allows up to four levels in a hierarchical format, such as clients, tasks, projects, or descriptions. You can also apply tags if you need to categorize items further. There are more settings related to the workspace, but these are more general, such as changing the currency, workspace cost rate, billable rate, or your team's working days.

Another feature you might want to set up is time rounding. This is linked to time entries, and you need to decide if you want it rounded up, down, or to the nearest whole number. You can also review and approve any team member's time.

Tracking Work Hours

To start tracking time, you need to open Clockify, enter the task you are doing, and start the timer. When you stop or begin working on another task, you can simply stop the timer, enter a new activity, and begin the tracker once again. The previous tracker will be recorded, and you can have access to it at any time. You can even check the time tracked per week or month. You don't need to add a description when you start tracking your time; you can do it later, and the app will categorize it once you do. If you start working on the same task later, you just need to click on the timer to restart.

When you turn it off again, this time it will add to the one in the same category.

You may forget to turn on the tracker, but that's not a problem because you can change the starting time or manually change the time afterward.

Generating Reports

Reports are a great way to analyze where you've spent your time task-wise. These reports are so detailed that you can break down the data by description, project, or even by date or tag. There's a feature where you can filter data by project or tag, or choose between different time periods, check your habits, and how your productivity is progressing.

Rescue Time

Rescue Time is similar to Clockify in that its main function is to automate time tracking, with a unique feature: it blocks distractions. It also has AI incorporated into the software, which allows for many different functionalities. For example, your day starts with the app assistant's morning forecast where you can see your planned activities for the day, and receive timing suggestions for an uninterrupted focus session depending on your calendar.

Getting Started

The first thing you must do is download the app. There are two download options: one for Windows and another for Mac. The app also offers many walkthroughs, so you can get familiar with its features. After installation, you can start checking your tracked activities as Rescue Time tracks your app and browser activity. It will then start to send you reports on how you spend your time.

You can connect your calendar simply by clicking "Account Settings" and then "Calendar Integration." Depending on the calendar you're using, there are different ways to do it, but the software has tutorials on how you can integrate the different calendars. Then, you can open the assistant, and you will get reminders for any upcoming meetings. Meetings have a dedicated page, but they are inserted into your calendar. With an easy-to-read graph, you can also see how many meetings are taking time away from your work.

You should also set up your work schedule so you can get better results and for the app to start recording your time. You can also categorize your tasks and activities by "Focus Work," "Other Work,", or "Personal Activities." Then you just need to go to the "Activities Page" to check how much time you've spent on each. As you might have guessed, depending on the category of tasks, some rank higher than others. For instance, "Focus Work" is the most important task, while "Other Work" ranks second and might include sending emails and any other administrative work. Lastly, "Personal Activities" are non-work activities and rank last in order of priority.

With the feature "Focus sessions," you can block out any websites or apps on your computer that most negatively impact your focus. This is quite a useful feature for when you need long periods without any interruptions and you need to fully focus on what you are doing.

Setting Goals

Goals in Rescue Time are there to enhance your habits at work. You can simply go to the menu and click on Goals, where you have a plethora of different goal options. The "Focus Work" goals incorporate your meetings and other information and generate a daily goal for your "Focus Work." Then, there's the "Distraction and Communication" goal that helps you avoid multitasking and focus on not losing your workflow.

The "Recommended Goals for Focus Sessions" are simply goals for a day that keep you on your toes about completing the necessary activities you must do during that day. Lastly, the "Balance" goals monitor how much work you do outside your working schedule and give you reports on it.

Toggl

Toggl is an app that lets you track how much time you spend on activities. It's mostly used by freelancers who need to track activities for their billable hours, but it's also popular with students and with those who want to improve their productivity.

Toggl works online in a browser, but you can also install it on your computer or phone and track time from there. Users report the app as being user friendly and has a straightforward interface.

Features:

Time Tracking. You can track time by using a timer, entering it manually, or adding your calendar events as time entries. The app even has offline tracking, time tracking reminders, and idle detection.

Integrations. You can track time in tools that you already use. Installing the browser extension embeds the Toggl Track timer into the user interface of the online app so you can start the timer without switching tabs.

Reporting. Toggl has three types of reports: (1) Summary, where you can review total tracked time and apply filters; (2) Detailed, where you can see each individual time entry; and (3) Weekly, where you can review tracked time throughout the week.

Project Management. While requiring more manual input, Toggl is reliable for project tracking and allows setting time-based project budgets with email alerts when projects near or exceed these budgets. Additionally, Toggl provides basic project management features, such as task creation and team assignment.

Getting Started

New users can sign up for free at https://accounts.toggl.com/track/signup/ using an email address, Google, or Apple account.

Toggl is free for up to 5 team members. If you're an individual who just wants to know where your time goes, the basic free version is all you need.

FINANCIAL TOOLS AND APPS

Financial tools and apps can assist with budgeting, expense tracking, financial planning, invoicing, and billing. These tools enhance efficiency and productivity, with their usefulness varying based on the specific tasks and responsibilities of your role as a virtual assistant.

Quickbooks

Quickbooks is one of the best apps when it comes to sending invoices, quotes, and anything related to accounting, especially for small businesses. With this tool, you can do away with using spreadsheets or manual bookkeeping. There's more to Quickbooks aside from its accounting functions, such as payroll, commerce (inventory dashboard), everything being saved in the cloud, the ability to generate payment-enabled invoices, and even tracking billable hours.

Keep in mind that these are different services, and while they are an option, you can just stick to what you need and don't necessarily have to sign up for all of them.

Setting Up

The first thing you need to do is sign up for the accounting software on this link: https://quickbooks.intuit.com/# You also must add Quickbooks Live so you can fully customize your dashboard. Everything works seamlessly. If you need to add team members who must be paid through Quickbooks, you can easily add Quickbooks payroll and employees.

Invoicing

Invoicing is one of the most important features in Quickbooks. You can create invoices from scratch, from an estimate, or even set them up for recurrent payments. Sending invoices have never been easier; you can set up automated invoice sending using your client's email address, or you can print the physical invoice for mailing to the client's address.

Tax Calculations

The best feature of Quickbooks is its easy taxation functionality. The software is one of the easiest to use when calculating your taxes because it already has a record of your income and expenses and performs calculations automatically. This feature even extends to the payroll service.

You can also upload receipts into the system if you use the mobile app and take a picture of the receipt, so you don't have to collect them all and input them into the system yourself.

Freshbooks

Freshbooks is a similar tool to Quickbooks, and while it has similar functions, it also has some differences.

Getting Started

To get started with Freshbooks, you first need to sign up for an account. There is also have a 30-day trial with all the features included, enabling you to try out the application prior to purchasing. First, you need to sign up through the Freshbooks official page, enter your email, and register a password. After registration, you need to click on the "Getting Started" button. If you're using an iPhone or a Mac, you still need to go to the company's official page, but select "Sign in with Apple." Then you must enter your Apple ID, email, and password and verify via a two-factor authentication. The final step is account verification, completion of which will enable you to use the software.

Steps for setting up with an Android or a Google account is similar to the previous process, with the only difference being the use your Google account details during registration.

Main Features

Freshbooks is perhaps the easiest accounting software to use. It also has a user-friendly mobile application to get things done on the go. Its tax filing is pretty straightforward. You can get a summary of your revenues, so it's even easier for you to report your income. It also has a great categorization system when it comes to expenses and generates reports, as well as introducing deductions when needed.

Its time-tracking feature is also a great functionality if you ever need to track your team's time. Its analytics and reporting are easy to generate and understand, and it can give you a summary of sales tax, invoice details, and expense reports.

Wave

Wave is a simple accounting software with free cloud storage where you can store your files.

Getting Started

First, you need to sign up with your email address, or alternatively, you can use a Google account. Once that is done, you can start to set up the software. You will then be prompted to create a business space, and each can be a different client. At this stage, you also must specify the type of organization you work for, your name, the country in which you company was established, and your preferred currency.

Main Features

Wave is free to use with no costs or charges. One advantage of the Wave is its strong invoicing feature. The only downside is that the program has fewer features and functions compared to the other two software programs on this list. It also has limited integration, but the basic functionalities in the program will most likely be enough to start with if you are not currently intending to pay for an accounting software.

INVENTORY STEPS

Clockify

Getting Started

1. Visit Clockify's website and sign up for a free account using your email address.
2. Choose a plan, starting with the free version. Upgrade options are available.

3. Once signed in, a workspace is automatically created. Add more workspaces if needed.
4. In profile settings, add personal information, preferences, and a picture.
5. Set up workspace settings, including time-tracking data, categorization levels, and additional preferences.
6. Configure time-rounding preferences.
7. Optionally, review and approve team members' time entries.

Tracking Work Hours

1. Open Clockify, enter the task description, and start the timer.
2. Stop the timer when done or switch to another task, entering new activities as needed.
3. View and manage time entries, categorized by task descriptions, projects, or clients.

Generating Reports

1. Access detailed reports on time spent, categorized by description, project, date, or tag.
2. Filter the data by project, tag, or time.
3. Analyze productivity trends using graphical representations.

Rescue Time

Getting Started

1. Download the Rescue Time app for Windows or Mac.
2. Install the app and follow walkthroughs to familiarize yourself.

3. Connect your calendar through "Account Settings" for meeting reminders.
4. Set up a work schedule and categorize tasks into "Focus Work," "Other Work," or "Personal Activities."

Setting Goals

1. Navigate to the "Goals" section in the menu.
2. Set goals for "Focus Work," "Distraction and Communication," and other recommended focus sessions.
3. Monitor progress and receive reports on your work habits.

Focus Sessions

1. Use "Focus Sessions" to block distractions during extended work periods.
2. Configure settings to block websites or apps, ensuring uninterrupted focus.

Toggl

Getting Started

1. Download the Toggl app for desktop or mobile.
2. Sign up for Toggl Track by entering your email address, or by using your Google or Apple account.
3. Add your team members by clicking on the Organization tab on the left-hand menu, then click "Invite Members" on the top right corner. Invite members by adding in their email address.
4. Create projects to assign time entries to by clicking on "Projects" on the left-hand menu and by clicking "+ New Project" on the top right corner.

5. Create tags to add to your time entries by clicking on "Tags" on the left-hand menu and "+ New Tag" on the top right corner.

6. Start tracking time by clicking the pink play button after selecting a project and/or tag and hitting the stop button once finished.

7. Click on the Reports Tab on the left-hand menu to view different types of reports. You can choose the level of details you wish to view such as total tracked time, detailed view of each individual time entry, or total tracked time by the week.

Quickbooks

Setting Up

1. Sign up for Quickbooks accounting software.
2. Add Quickbooks Live for customized dashboard features.
3. Incorporate Quickbooks payroll if team members need to be paid through Quickbooks.

Invoicing

1. Create invoices from scratch, make estimates, or set up recurring payments.
2. Send invoices to clients via email or print them for physical delivery.

Tax Calculations

1. Leverage Quickbooks for easy tax calculations.
2. Upload receipts through the mobile app for convenient record-keeping.

Freshbooks

Getting Started

1. Sign up for an account on the Freshbooks official page.
2. Use a 30-day trial to explore all features.
3. Sign in with Apple for iOS users or use Google account details for Android users.

Main Features

1. Utilize the user-friendly mobile application for on-the-go tasks.
2. Simplify tax filing with straightforward summaries of revenues and expenses.
3. Track time for team members, generate analytics reports, and manage sales tax.

Wave

Getting Started

1. Sign up with your email address or Google account.
2. Create a business space and specify organization details.

Main Features

1. Utilize the free cloud storage.
2. Set up business spaces for different clients.
3. Specify the organization type, name, country, and preferred currency.

THE LEAP OF FAITH

"The best way to predict the future is to create it."

— ABRAHAM LINCOLN

At this stage in our journey, when you may be feeling a little overwhelmed, I'd like to refer you back to the foreword of this book. As you may remember, I transitioned to remote work from a traditional 9 to 5 job. While my expertise in the VA arena may come not from taking this route for myself but from becoming a VA employer, my journey may still look similar to yours.

I know what that doubt is like at the beginning, the giant leap of faith you must take to walk away from a secure and steady income, and I also know that it is possible. For a VA, the road is arguably even more secure. As many sectors face threats from the evolution of technology, the demand for virtual assistants is only increasing. The rise of remote work has truly been a blessing for the opportunities available to VAs, and it makes the dream of a flexible and lucrative career even more of a possibility. Your key tool is your determination to succeed; everything you're learning here is important, but ultimately, it will be your drive that pushes you to success.

As someone who's come this far and is already looking for practical strategies, I know you have that drive, and I'd like to ask you to use it to inspire someone else. For many people, the idea of career flexibility and financial freedom is nothing more than a dream. They don't truly believe it's possible or within their power to go out and get it. Just as I hope my own story will inspire you, your story can be an inspiration to someone else.

By leaving a review of this book on Amazon, you'll help other people find this 7-day guide and show them that it is within their reach.

In the era of remote work, designing your own life has become a real possibility for so many people who would otherwise feel stuck. The challenge now is showing them this; your review could make a huge difference.

Thank you so much for your support. As you know, the guidance of those who've trodden the path before you is crucial when you're beginning a new chapter in your life.

"Scan the QR code below to leave your review on Amazon"

CHAPTER FIVE

A VA'S GUIDE TO BUILDING AN INCREDIBLE PORTFOLIO

Creating an effective and attractive portfolio is crucial for attracting clients and building your online presence. Consider your portfolio as your passport to professional opportunities. Having an effective portfolio is an excellent way to increase your chances of getting hired or landing a project, as this can help your clients better understand your skills and expertise.

Let's get started on how you can build an incredible portfolio.

SHOWCASE YOUR SKILLS

First, you need to identify your niche and target market. This is vital so you know what work samples you can add to your portfolio. Consider the types of services you plan to offer as a VA, your ideal clients, and your primary goals. This will help you curate samples that are relevant to the jobs you want. For example, you might include like executive or entrepreneurial virtual assistance, digital marketing, social media management, podcast support, or general VA tasks.

When selecting your samples, prioritize quality over quantity. Focus on showcasing projects that highlight your skills and your relevant achievements. If your strengths are increasing client conversions or traffic, illustrate these accomplishments clearly. Additionally, demonstrate your adaptability and versatility, as these are key traits for VAs. Including diverse samples will show potential employers your ability to handle various tasks and challenges.

To enhance your professionalism, you can organize your portfolio by categories or themes. This structure makes it a lot easier for potential employers to review your portfolio and reflects your organization skills, a highly valued quality in VAs. Regularly update your portfolio to present a comprehensive view of your competencies, newly acquired skills, and relevant experiences, increasing your chances of getting hired.

How to Organize Your Portfolio

While organizing your portfolio by high-level themes or categories is a great start, diving deeper into organization can offer more advantages.

Begin by deciding on your niche and the services you intend to provide. This involves profiling your ideal clients so you can design your portfolio towards the services and skills they are most likely seeking.

Include work samples even if you're just starting out. For instance, if you aim to provide website creation services, create a website for yourself and use that as a sample in your portfolio. This will help demonstrate your capabilities effectively.

Ensure that potential clients can easily contact you. While it may seem obvious, many new VAs overlook adding their contact details to their portfolios.

Choose a portfolio layout that suits your preferences and the services you offer. For content-writing VAs, a text-only portfolio might be most appropriate. Alternatively, a visual-only portfolio can be more visually-appealing and eye-catching. You can use graphics, screenshots, or any other illustrated media, however, images alone may not fully convey your message. Therefore, consider a combined text and visual layout with descriptive text accompanying images. Include titles and links to your best and most relevant work for clarity and impact.

Case Studies

Including case studies in your portfolio can effectively showcase how your services have addressed client specific needs. To create impactful case studies, start by detailing the situation, problem, or need. Then, explain your role in resolving the issue, including the steps you took, tools or resources you utilized, and the solutions you implemented. Conclude with a thorough description of the outcome and any relevant details.

Select case studies from various types of relevant work you've done, such as paid or unpaid projects, employment-based tasks, freelance gigs, or volunteer efforts. These examples should highlight your ability to effectively handle tasks and challenges and deliver results. If possible, obtain permission to use your client's real name or company name; otherwise, anonymize the details. Each case study should capture your skills and strengths, describe the client and their goals, detail task and project needs, and outline the challenges you overcame.

Ensure that the title of each case study is brief but descriptive. Adding relevant images, including the client's logo or likeness with authorization, can make your case studies more compelling.

Testimonials

Testimonials are crucial for boosting your online presence and credibility in a competitive world. They act as social proof, enhancing trust and increasing your chances of getting hired.

Collect testimonials by encouraging satisfied clients to leave reviews on various platforms, and then link these reviews to your website. You can also collaborate with social media influencers to post positive reviews of your services.

There are six main types of social proof: customer testimonials, expert endorsements, friend referrals, ratings and reviews, social media proof, and certifications. Customer testimonials and case studies are particularly impactful. In fields requiring expert opinions, such as medical or pharmaceutical sectors, endorsements from recognized professionals can significantly boost your credibility. Friend referrals, ratings, reviews, and social media proof are also valuable. Additionally, certifications from reputable organizations can enhance your portfolio's credibility.

Updating Your Portfolio

Regularly updating your portfolio is essential as you gain more experience and skills. Aim to update it every three to six months to keep your projects are relevant and current. Attach a resume to provide potential clients with a comprehensive view of your background and achievements.

Focus on adding and updating case studies and projects that align with the work you seek and the you want to attract. Tailor your portfolio to a specific niche or ideal client type will make it more effective. Always include completion dates of projects to ensure timeliness and relevance. Revamp old descriptions or sections to keep your portfolio fresh.

CREATING A PORTFOLIO WHEN YOU DON'T HAVE EXPERIENCE

There are several ways to build a portfolio if you are just starting and lack experience. You can create your own website or writing content for personal blogs, provided the work is professional and is relevant. Decide on the services you want to offer or the role you aim to fill, and develop projects that demonstrate your capabilities.

Another strategy is to create a mock client with a fictional background and company, showcasing projects that illustrate your skills.

Participating in challenges or competitions on freelancing websites can also provide valuable experience, even if you don't get hired.

Volunteering is another option, offering real work to include in your portfolio while gaining experience.

INTERACTIVE ELEMENTS

Now that you have learned the steps to build your portfolio, start working on each section outlined in this chapter. If you're just starting out, creating projects as you progress through this chapter will help you develop a comprehensive portfolio.

Building an impressive portfolio crucial for getting noticed and securing work as a virtual assistant. In the next chapter, we will discuss self-marking and self-promotion, essential for attracting more clients.

KEY TAKEAWAYS

In Chapter 5, we explored how to build a VA portfolio. Your portfolio is your passport to numerous opportunities. Identify your niche and your target market tailor your portfolio accordingly, showcasing quality work samples relevant to the jobs you aim for.

Organize your portfolio by categories to highlight your skills, keeping your ideal client in mind. Include case studies and testimonials to provide social proof of your accomplishments, and encourage satisfied clients to leave positive reviews.

Remember, a portfolio is a dynamic document that should be updated every three to six months to stay relevant. Even if you lack experience, create a portfolio by developing mock projects that demonstrate your skills. A well-crafted portfolio is vital for becoming a successful VA and can open doors to many opportunities.

PORTFOLIO TEMPLATE

Roles, tasks, and duties	Template	
Social media manager strategies	Generation of reports Analyzing performance metrics Monitor social media channels Curate engaging content for all kinds of platforms Schedule posts	(Add your skills)
Digital Marketing	Optimize SEO content Create email marketing campaigns Create digital marketing strategies	(Add your skills)
Executive VA	Conduct research Create and proofread emails Manage calendar	(Add your skills)
Experience	Template	
Previous organizations	Name of the organization: Johnson & Johnson Duration: Oct 2019 – Jun 2020 Role: Social Media Manager	(Add your experience)

	Responsibilities: Increase social media engagement through strategic content	
	Name of the organization: Freelancing experience Duration: Jul 2019 - present Services provided: Digital marketing, social media management	(Add your experience)
Testimonials	**Template**	
Past testimonials	John Smith, Johnson & Johnson: "Working with Tim has been a game-changer for my business. Their organization and efficiency had a direct impact on the company's productivity.	(Add your testimonials)
	Sarah Harris, Zara: I highly recommend Tim if you are looking for a great VA. He's extremely organized and always delivers quality work.	(Add your testimonials)
Case Studies	**Template**	
Project: Social Media Campaign	Overview: Came up with a two-month-long social media	(Add your case study)

for Johnson & Johnson	campaign to promote a new service launch.	
	Challenges: Limited awareness of the service.	(Add your case study)
	Solutions: Developed engaging content, and ran targeted ads.	(Add your case study)
	Outcome: Increased product visibility, resulting in a 30% sales boost.	(Add your case study)
Niche and Target Clients	**Template**	
Niche: Digital Marketing	Offering great services in digital marketing.	(Add your niche)
Target Clients	Small to medium-sized businesses seeking efficient social media management	(Add your target clients)

CHAPTER SIX

A VA'S GUIDE TO SELF-MARKETING

To thrive in a competitive industry, you need an effective strategy to make yourself known. If you don't brand yourself, others will. In this chapter, we will cover the essentials of personal branding and marketing, providing a blueprint for a self-marketing campaign that you can follow.

PERSONAL BRANDING

As a virtual assistant, personal branding is crucial. Unlike employees of a firm, you must market yourself, as you are essentially your own business. Effective self-promotion can be the difference between securing clients or not in a competitive market. A strong personal brand builds a positive professional reputation, attracts ideal clients, and enhances your market visibility.

What is a Personal Brand?

Personal branding is about establishing your unique identity. Just like companies such as Pepsi or McDonald's, your brand should evoke specific associations.

As a VA, the first step is defining your brand identity, including your values, mission, skills, and strengths. This foundation allows you to present a consistent and authentic message across all platforms.

Consistency is key. Your message, presentation, and visual elements should align with your brand identity across different platforms. This includes using professional headshots or logos, consistent color schemes, and readable, on-brand fonts. For example, if your website features orange tones, use the same hues on all your platforms and even in your office décor.

Crafting Your Message

Your message is a primary vehicle for showcasing your brand. It should be consistent and reflect your brand identity. Highlight your accomplishments, connect with others in the industry, and share insights. When networking, ensure your communication always remains on-brand.

Visual elements also play a significant role. Whether you use a professional headshot or a logo, consistency in colors and fonts across platforms reinforces your brand. Choose colors that resonate with your values, as different hues evoke different emotions. Similarly, select a font that aligns with your brand's tone, whether modern, classic, or minimalist.

Authenticity and Storytelling

Authenticity is vital. Your brand should reflect your true self, not an imitation of someone else. Genuine communication, client testimonials, and sharing personal stories can enhance your authenticity.

While maintaining professionalism, let your audience see the human side of you. Owning up to mistakes and viewing them as learning opportunities also builds trust.

Storytelling is an effective way to connect with your audience. Share your journey, including why you became a VA, the challenges you overcame, and your passion for helping clients. Highlight your values and mission through your stories, making your brand relatable and compelling.

Unique Value Proposition (UVP)

Your UVP is a key component of your brand, outlining what sets you apart. Tailor your UVP to your niche audience, addressing their pain points and challenges. Demonstrate proficiency in the latest technology and VA tools, showcasing your ability to meet clients' needs with a personalized approach.

Here's an example UVP:

"I'm an experienced VA specializing in social media management. I bring creativity and strategy to help expand your business' online presence. With a customized approach for every client, I ensure authenticity, leading to higher online engagement and brand loyalty. I have a strong track record of successful completed projects, and I'm proficient in the latest technologies to improve every aspect of your social media world."

Tailor this example to fit your unique skills and audience, incorporating all elements of your brand vision.

Websites to Build Your Brand

Social media platforms are powerful marketing tools, however, having your own website gives your profile professionalism, branding, content, search engine visibility, and data insights.

The following website builders can help those with no web design experience or skills in creating their own website:

- Wix
- Squarespace
- Webify
- WordPress
- Siteground
- Weebly

Social Media Presence

While numerous social media platforms exist, three are indispensable for self-promotion: LinkedIn, Facebook, and Instagram. LinkedIn is especially important due to its professional focus. Let's explore how to effectively promote your business on these platforms.

Identifying Your Niche

Identifying your niche is crucial. Understanding your target is the first step in promoting your business and services. Choose the right channels and platforms based on where your potential clients are most active. Conduct thorough research to determine where your audience spends their time online.

Addressing Client Problems

Once you've identified your niche, focus on your potential client's problems and how you can solve them. Highlighting your past clients' challenges and how you helped them can be particularly effective. Many potential clients may not even realize they need a VA, but by showcasing how you've addressed similar issues, you can attract their interest. Your content should cater to their needs, such as achieving a better work-life balance, improving time management, or increasing productivity, even if they are not yet aware of these needs.

Creating Consistent Content

Building your brand on social media platforms involves more than occasional posts; consistency is key. Develop a regular posting schedule to build trust with clients, potential clients, and followers. Use a mix of videos, blog posts, and other engaging content. Remember to use hashtags to increase the visibility of your VA services.

By strategically using LinkedIn, Facebook, and Instagram, consistently addressing client needs, and maintaining a regular posting schedule, you can effectively promote your business and build a strong online presence.

NETWORKING

Networking can significantly increase your chances of finding work. This chapter explores various networking strategies, both online and offline, that can help you build valuable connections in your industry.

Online Opportunities

The internet offers a wealth of networking opportunities through online communities, which are the easiest ways to start connecting with others in your field. These communities, found on social media platforms, blogs, podcasts, forums, and newsletters, are filled with people who share your interests, potential clients, and industry peers. Engaging in these online spaces provides valuable insights, feedback, resources, and general support from people who understand your work. Online communities are also excellent avenues to showcase your skills and experience.

You can also attend virtual meetings tailored to professionals in your industry on platforms such as Zoom, Eventbrite, and Meetup. These events not only facilitate networking but also opportunities to learn about new trends and acquire new skills.

Offline Opportunities

For those who prefer face-to-face interactions, numerous offline networking opportunities exist. Joining your local chamber of commerce is an excellent way to meet business owners who might need your services. Remember, these events are for building relationships, not for direct selling. They can also provide information about trade shows, conferences, and seminars.

Professional clubs and meetup groups are also valuable resources. Look for groups that focus on business owners or other areas of interest. The key is to make genuine connections first and offer your services when appropriate.

The Elevator Pitch

The elevator pitch is a concise yet persuasive speech that highlights what you do and your experience. It's an excellent tool for quickly capturing the attention of potential clients and making a memorable impression. Ideally, your pitch should convey your key message within thirty seconds. Additionally, it's a valuable asset for networking, allowing you to effectively introduce yourself in various professional settings.

While many people have a general idea of what a VA does, their understanding might not be entirely accurate or complete due to the diverse roles VAs can play. When crafting an elevator pitch, it's important to clearly define your services and the value you can provide to potential clients. Begin by providing a brief summary of your services, emphasizing key points you want your audience to remember. Maintain enthusiasm throughout your pitch to make a lasting impression. Additionally, highlight your unique selling proposition by explaining what sets your services apart from others. This distinction is essential in conveying why clients should choose you over the competition. By the end of your pitch, your audience should have a clear understanding of what you offer and how it can benefit them.

Memorize your pitch and ensure that you practice consistently until you have mastered the entire piece. Mastery will lead to effortless and natural delivery, suggesting sincerity during your presentation.

Freelance Platforms

There are several freelancing platforms, each with its own specialization. It is essential to build a detailed and complete profile on each platform. A professional-looking profile will make you stand out from the competition. Make sure to include a professional picture, a short bio, your experience, and work samples. Most importantly, highlight your strengths effectively. Wherever possible, link to your external portfolio on your website to enhance your professional image.

Being proactive and completing numerous projects is crucial, as it positively impacts your profile. The more projects you complete, the more positive reviews you will receive, which in turn will attract additional work. Below is a list of some of the most popular freelancing platforms to consider:

- Fiverr
- Upwork
- Toptal
- Freelancer.com
- Flexjobs
- Guru
- LinkedIn
- People Per Hour

Note that each platform caters to different skills and service categories, and may even be more suitable for specific project types. For example, Upwork is a great place to build long-term business relationships, while Fiverr is often associated with shorter-term projects.

Cold Outreach

Cold outreach could be an effective but often challenging way to connect with potential clients. It typically involves researching leads and sending introductory emails.

There two types of leads - warm leads and cold leads. A warm lead is someone you've already interacted with. You might already know them or have at least spoken to them at some point. A cold lead is someone with whom you have had no prior contact.

To succeed in cold outreach, you need to cultivate the right mindset. Keep in mind that you are not asking for money; you're offering valuable services to someone who might need them. Start by identifying potential clients. Do you know any business owners who might benefit from your services? Check your social media; you might already be following business owners or be on some mailing lists. It is recommended to start with businesses that you are familiar with to come across as authentic.

Researching about the company you're reaching out to is crucial. Before sending your pitch, review their website, follow them on social media, read their blogs—do anything to familiarize yourself with their business. This shows that you care about their company, and if you get hired, it will make it easier to get started.

When writing your pitch, answer questions that business owners might have before interacting with you. Demonstrate that you understand their business. Include details about how you discovered their company, explain how you can add value, and describe how your services can improve their business, product, or service.

Add a call to action, inviting them to respond or book a meeting. Lastly, include your rates; listing your hourly rate is usually sufficient. Make sure your email covers the following points:

- Your name
- The services you offer
- How or where you found them
- How your expertise can help their business
- A call to action
- And a warm closing

Follow-Up Strategy

If you do not get a response, you can send a follow-up email after a few days. avoid spamming them daily. Keep the follow up shorter than your initial email since you've already provided all the essential information. Offer additional value, such as an initial discount or a trial period (one small project, for example). Be persistent but not pushy, as being overly aggressive is a sure-fire way to not get a response.

SUMMARY

When building your brand, ensure you do the following:

- A complete LinkedIn profile

  o Choose a good and professional picture
  o Optimize your headline
  o Work on your summary
  o If possible, add visual content

- Make your profile SEO-friendly (so potential clients can easily find you).
- Know your unique point of view
- Post consistently
- Be authentic
- Focus on your expertise
- Invest in your brand.

Self-promotion is a crucial aspect of being a VA and doing it effectively can help you secure work from the get-go. It takes time, but it is essential, particularly when you are just starting out and lack extensive experience.

SEO-FRIENDLY PROFILE

Making your profile SEO-friendly is essential for ranking higher on search engines and reaching more potential customers. Here are some steps make sure that your profile is optimized:

Keyword Research

Start with thorough keyword research. Understand your niche and identify the specific services you offer. Think from the client's perspective—what keywords are they likely to use when searching for a VA?

Natural Keyword Integration

Ensure that the keywords flow naturally throughout your profile. Use a strong primary keyword in your headline along with related terms that describe your services. In the skills section, list your relevant skills using both main keywords and any related variations. Your summary should highlight not only your skills but also your experience, incorporating relevant keywords seamlessly.

Niche-Specific Terms

Emphasize niche-specific terms. Clearly describe the services you provide, using industry terminology to help potential candidates find you. Showcase your achievements and results, introducing keywords in your case studies and encouraging clients to use keywords in their testimonials and recommendations.

Optimized Titles and Job Descriptions

Optimize your job titles and job descriptions to include keywords related to your roles. Regularly update your profile to reflect the latest trends and developments in your industry.

LinkedIn SEO Features

Leverage LinkedIn's SEO features. Populate your skills and endorsements with prioritized keywords, allowing LinkedIn's algorithm to match your profile effectively. Customize your public profile URL to include your name but also any relevant keywords for visibility.

KEY TAKEAWAYS

Building an effective personal brand involves understanding your audience and shaping your identity around it. By defining your values, mission, and skills, maintaining consistency across platforms, and staying authentic, you can create a compelling personal brand that attracts ideal clients and sets you apart in the market. Use the template provided to outline your personal branding vision and incorporate these principles into your strategy.

Having a personal website secures your online presence, serving as a central hub for your professional identity. Equally important is maintaining active and engaging social media profiles. Make efforts to consistently post relevant content to attract more followers and build trust with your audience.

Networking is crucial for VAs and can be done both online and offline. Offline networking includes attending conferences and seminars related to your field, which provide opportunities to meet potential clients and peers. Online networking offers even more options, as it is not restricted by geographical location. You can join online communities, forums, blogs, and other digital platforms to connect with others in your industry.

Honing your elevator pitch is essential. This brief, 30-second introduction should clearly convey who you are and what services you offer, highlighting what makes you unique. Practicing your pitch will ensure you can deliver it confidently and effectively when the opportunity arises.

Building profiles on freelancing platforms like Upwork or Fiverr is vital for increasing your visibility and potential earnings. These platforms connect you with clients looking for your specific skills set.

Cold emailing potential clients can be daunting, but it opens doors to new opportunities. When done thoughtfully, it can lead to responses and even projects. After an interview or initial contact, employ a follow-up strategy. If you don't receive a response within a few days, send a polite follow-up email. Be persistent but not pushy, as this balance is key to maintaining professionalism and respect.

By integrating these strategies, you can effectively promote your services, build a strong professional network, and enhance your chances of securing more projects and clients.

ELEVATOR PITCH TEMPLATE

Hi, I'm (Your Name), an experienced VA passionate about boosting business efficiency and productivity. With a background in (Your Relevant Experience and Education), I bring a strategic approach to handling administrative tasks. I specialize in providing comprehensive support to ensure seamless business operations, allowing you to focus on making crucial decisions about your business.

COLD OUTREACH TEMPLATE

Dear (Recipient's Name),

I hope this email finds you well. My name is (Your Name), and I'm a skilled Virtual Assistant (VA) dedicated to enhancing businesses like yours. I am keenly aware about the challenges of managing multiple tasks in today's fast-paced world. With my specialization in (Your Services and Niche), I can streamline your operations and improve overall efficiency.

Here are a few ways my skills can benefit your business:

- **Flexibility**: I adapt to various business environments and am willing to adjust to schedules and arrangements according to your business needs and operations.
- **Professionalism**: I maintain high standards of professionalism in my work. I am mindful of deadlines, have a sense of urgency, employ tact and discretion in my communications, and respect authority.
- **Advanced Time Management**: I use advanced time management strategies, such as (Time Management Tools), to prioritize tasks efficiently.
- **Efficient Task Management**: I'm an efficient task manager who can handle multiple tasks - projects, calendars, emails, and more - without compromising quality or timely delivery.

I would appreciate an opportunity to discuss how my expertise can align with your business needs. Could we schedule a brief call at your convenience? Thank you for considering my application, and I look forward to the possibility of contributing to the success of (insert business name).

Regards,

(Your Name)

(Your Contact Details)

(Y Portfolio and/or LinkedIn Profile)

PERSONAL BRANDING VISION TEMPLATE

Authenticity		
	Core Values	**Authentic Traits**
List your core values and authentic traits		
Storytelling		
	Examples	**Your Examples**
Origin Story	Here you must briefly narrate your path to becoming a VA	
Values and Mission	Detail your values and mission that drives you to do better as a VA	
Client Success	Emphasize success stories when helping your clients	

Unique Approach	Talk about the unique approach that you use as a professional VA	
Milestones	Share milestones throughout your career.	
Challenges	Share a story where you had difficulties to overcome	
Visual Identity		
	Examples	**Your Examples**
Colors	Pick a color palette reflecting your brand	
Style	Define your visual style	
Fonts	Choose a font that aligns with your brand and style	
Logo	Create a logo that shows what your brand is about (or a headshot)	
Office Imagery	Understand what your brand is and transport it to your physical space	

Website Aesthetics	Write down the aesthetics you want to convey on your website	

CHAPTER SEVEN

HOW TO FIND EMPLOYMENT OPPORTUNITIES AS A VA

"Opportunity doesn't make appointments. You have to be ready when it arrives."

— TIM FARGO

I f you know where and how to look for work as a VA, you will discover numerous opportunities. In this chapter, we will explore effective strategies for identifying and securing these opportunities, ensuring you find jobs that align with your skills and career goals.

JOB BOARDS

Job boards are a valuable resource for finding VA opportunities, and they come in two types: specialized and general. Specialized job boards focus on virtual assistant roles, offering more targeted results, while general job boards provide a broader range of listings but may not be as specific to your niche.

When looking for jobs on these boards, using the right keywords is crucial. Simply searching for "virtual assistant" might not yield the best results, especially if you have specialized skills. Instead, use keywords related to your niche or specific companies you are interested in working with. Most job boards have search filters that can help narrow down your search to find the perfect job.

Before diving into the different job boards, let's first recap some key points for being a successful VA. As highlighted throughout this book, having the right mindset is crucial. Finding the best client for you is essentially a numbers game, requiring persistence and consistency. Having a strong pitch is also crucial. While most job boards facilitate the connection between businesses and virtual assistants, having a polished pitch ready is always beneficial. Follow-ups, similar to cold emails, can significantly increase your chances of getting hired.

Now let's look at some of the best job boards on the web.

Top Job Boards

Freelancer.com: Considered to be one of the best online marketplaces for freelancing jobs, it's completely free to sign up and offers opportunities across various industries.

Upwork: A great platform for connecting with potential clients, however, getting your profile approved requires effort. Upwork screens your resume, work samples, case studies, rates, and personal statement during the approval process.

LinkedIn ProFinder: Part of LinkedIn, this segment is dedicated to connecting freelancers with job opportunities. It's a reputable and extensive network for professional connections.

Monster: A classic job board that is free to use and user-friendly, making it easy to get started on your job search.

Guru: Tailored for VAs with specific skills in design, sales and marketing, engineering, legal, programming, business and finance, or administrative and secretarial jobs.

Indeed: Not only a robust search engine for jobs, but also an excellent platform with numerous job listings. It's also free to use.

COMPANY WEBSITES

Going directly to company websites is another effective strategy, especially if you're targeting specific industries like e-commerce, healthcare, or tech. Some companies are known for regularly hiring VAs. Here are a few examples:

Beacon Hill Staffing Group: A staffing solutions company that focuses on part-time or temporary work in various sectors, including legal. Contacting them often leads to direct hire opportunities.

CVS Health: This healthcare company frequently posts job listings for virtual and remote positions on their website, making it a great resource for VA opportunities in the healthcare industry.

Equivity: While specialized in legal services, Equivity also hires in other different fields such as marketing.

Great Assist: Previously known as Profit Factory, this HR services company provides general and administrative VA roles.

* * *

When searching for companies, there are several strategies you can use to improve your chances of being hired for the type of work you want. Start by exploring the career or jobs section on the websites mentioned earlier. These sections often list job openings that align with your profile.

One effective technique is to tailor your resume to each job application. While this may be time-consuming, it can significantly enhance your prospects. Begin by researching and understanding what the company does. Then, update your skills section and customize your job history to highlight relevant experiences.

When sending unsolicited job applications, it's crucial to conduct thorough research on the company. Tailor your application to the specific role, address it to the appropriate person, and clearly showcase your skills. After submitting your application, send a follow-up email to express your continued interest in the position.

If you are responding to an employment ad, carefully review the job description and tailor your application accordingly. Emphasize your achievements and ensure you follow the application instructions, as these can vary from one employer to another.

RECRUITMENT AGENCIES

When searching for a job, using recruitment agencies can be an effective strategy. These agencies work directly with companies seeking employees and individual clients who might be looking for VAs. Partnering with a recruitment agency can significantly increase your chances of landing a job, though it's important to understand the process involved.

First, there's the initial contact and screening. You'll need to reach out to your chosen recruitment agency and sign up. They might request for an in-person meeting or a virtual call via Zoom, for example. During this meeting you'll discuss details such as your CV, work history, and other relevant information. The agency will keep your CV on file, and when a suitable opportunity arises, they might forward it to potential clients. Additionally, when companies contact agencies, the agencies often post the job online and search through their existing applicant pool.

You can also proactively contact the agency if they list a job that interests you. If the agency finds you suitable for the role, you may be invited for an interview, as there will likely be other candidates in consideration. The agency may provide support throughout these stages to boost your chances of success.

There's usually no cost to the applicant, and recruitment agencies are compensated by the companies that hire their services.

Pros and Cons

One of the biggest advantages of using recruitment agencies to find a job is the faster hiring process. These agencies can efficiently match candidates' qualities with employers' needs, increasing the likelihood of a successful job pairing. Additionally, agencies often have connections that you may lack, particularly if you're new to the industry.

However, be aware that some agencies might not only be paid by the employer but may also take a cut from your salary, at least initially. Relying solely on recruitment agencies can limit your control over your job options, so it's crucial to conduct thorough research when job hunting. Ensure the agency you choose has a strong track record of working with VAs and a robust network of potential clients.

Here are some examples of agencies where you can look for VA opportunities:

- SINQ
- FlexJobs
- Virtual Coworker
- Boldly
- C Suites Assistants

FREELANCE GIGS

Being a VA opens you up to freelance work which is a great way to gain experience in diverse areas. As we will see, freelance work doesn't intrinsically mean short-term employment; there are many opportunities to work long-term as a freelancer.

Short-Term vs. Long-Term

Short-term freelance work is typically project-based, meaning you are hired for a specific project, and your role ends once the project is complete. The duration can range from a few weeks to several months, depending on the project's scope. Often, you will primarily interact with the project team, even if a larger company is involved. The short-term nature of these gigs allows you to take on multiple clients simultaneously, providing the opportunity to diversify your income, especially if each job lasts only a few weeks or less.

In contrast, long-term freelance gigs offer a more stable income but often require more hours and offer less flexibility. These roles usually extend beyond four to five months, though the exact duration can vary. While they can also be project-based, long-term gigs typically demand full-time commitment for the duration of the job. As a result, you may be limited to working with a single client due to the extensive hours required.

How to Secure Freelance Work

Chances are there will be a point in your VA career when you will need to find freelance work, even if you intend to pursue longer-term contracts. Landing your first freelance contract when you have no experience might be a little challenging. Below are some tips to help you in securing freelance work as a VA:

First, you must define your niche and services. To attract clients, you need a clear understanding of what you offer. By defining your niche and choosing the services you will provide, you can focus your search effectively. Identify what makes you unique, particularly your skills and expertise, to define your target audience precisely.

Next, create an impressive portfolio. Although discussed extensively in previous chapters, here's a brief summary: select samples of your best work, even if you have yet to take on a client. Build an online portfolio on your own website, showcasing self-initiated projects, case studies, and testimonials. Leverage your social media platforms such as Facebook and LinkedIn by sharing valuable content, which can drive traffic to your website and increase your chances of getting hired.

Earlier chapters listed some of the most common and popular freelance marketplaces. These are excellent starting points for finding your first gig. These platforms allow you to showcase your skills and connect with clients seeking VA services. Additionally, don't underestimate the power of networking and referrals. Attending industry events, joining groups, or participating in online forums can help you network with peers find clients.

Finally, prepare a compelling pitch for potential clients. Make it short, concise, and persuasive, highlighting your services and strengths while addressing the client's pain points.

CHECKLIST

Job Search Platforms

- LinkedIn
- Fiverr
- Freelancer.com
- Toptal

- People Per Hour
- Upwork
- Guru

Job Search Strategies

- Job boards
- Specialize and niche down
- Use social media
- Join VA communities
- Enhance your online presence
- Continue to update your skills
- Attend networking events

Following the strategies laid out in this chapter will aid you in your job search. The next chapter covers techniques on how to ace a job interview.

KEY TAKEAWAYS

Chapter 7 covers helpful tips on finding employment as a VA. First, we looked at the two categories of job boards: specialized and general. Specialized job boards list jobs for VAs with specialized niches such as healthcare and legal. General job boards are for more general and non-specialized VA work. Remember to use relevant keywords and apply filters when looking through these job boards. Some examples are Upwork, LinkedIn, Monster, and Indeed.

Visiting company websites can also prove useful when targeting open VA positions. You need to tailor your CV to the requirements of positions you are interested in to have a better chance of landing the job. In addition, you can also partner with recruitment agencies to broaden your job search initiatives.

Freelance gigs are the bread and butter of VAs especially for those who are just starting their VA careers. There are numerous free-lancing opportunities for both short- and long-term work, and gig seekers may opt to take on multiple short-term projects at the same time or consecutively.

When looking for work as a freelance VA you must first decide on the niche you wish to work in. You must also create an impressive portfolio to showcase your work, leverage social media, and network as much as possible to increase your chances of connecting with exciting work opportunities.

COVER LETTER TEMPLATE

(Your Name)

(Your Address)

(Your City, State, or ZIP code)

(Your Email Address)

(Your Phone Number)

(Date)

(Hiring Manager's Name)

(Company Name)

(Company Address)

(City, State, and ZIP code)

Dear (Hiring Manager's Name),

I'm writing to express my interest in the (Job Title) position at (Company Name), as advertised on (where you found the job). With extensive experience in (relevant industry and skills) and a proven track record of (any relevant achievements that relate to the job in question), I am confident that my skills and abilities will significantly contribute to your team and business.

In my previous role as (previous and relevant role) at (previous company), I successfully (describe relevant achievements). This experience enabled me to acquire (specific skills), which I believe can make a substantial impact at (Company Name).

Key skills that I bring include:

- (Relevant Skill)
- (Relevant Skill)
- (Relevant Skill)
- (Relevant Skill)

I am particularly drawn to (Company Name) because of its commitment to (insert company's values or mission). Your dedication to (specific achievements or initiatives of the company) aligns with my own professional values and aspirations.

I'm excited about the opportunity to contribute to (Company Name)'s success and would welcome a chance to discuss how my expertise can benefit your team. Thank you for considering my application, and I look forward to the possibility of an interview.

Regards,

(Your Name)

THE ONLY GUIDE YOU'LL EVER NEED FOR ACING A VA INTERVIEW

The interview is not just about being the right fit for the company, but also about letting the company be the right fit for you. Attending an interview can be both extremely exciting and terrifying, but ensuring that you are well prepared for the interview will boost your confidence, which in, turn can increase your chances of making a great first impression.

PREPARATION

Preparation for your interview is crucial. It reduces stress and enhances your performance. While you may have done some initial research when you applied, now you need to delve deeper. You must familiarize yourself with the company's products or services, their client base, and their core values. Understanding the company's goals, values, and culture allows you to tailor your responses effectively during the interview.

During the interview, you must continue to emphasize your skills and expertise even if those are detailed in your CV. The best VAs possess a diverse skill set, but it's always good practice to highlight traits such as flexibility, organization, clear communication, and time management skills. Additionally, improving your tech skills is important. Proficiency with current tools enhances your appeal as a VA and increases your chances of getting hired. Discuss your familiarity with time management software or communication tools. If you're not familiar with some of the tools they use, do quick research to show that you are a fast learner.

Being a great VA is not just about possessing hard skills; soft skills are equally important. Emphasize your communication and collaboration abilities, especially in remote settings. Highlight your problem-solving capabilities and your capacity to work independently, as these qualities can set you apart from other candidates.

Additionally, show enthusiasm and convey your excitement about the job. Ask insightful questions to demonstrate your genuine interest. However, be prepared to answer questions as well. Preparation is key, even if you don't know the exact questions you will be asked. Familiarize yourself with common interview questions to be better prepared and present yourself confidently. Here are some examples:

- What are your preferred administrative and communication tools and platforms?
- How do you juggle multiple assignments?
- What would your answer be if you couldn't meet a certain deadline?
- What if you don't fully understand what was assigned to you?
- Why do you want to be a virtual assistant?
- How would you deal with a particularly difficult client?

Formulate and practice your answers to the questions above. Research other possible questions that may be asked during the interview. Be prepared to answer job-specific and technical questions especially if the job you will be interviewing for belongs to a specific niche or industry.

Another frequently asked interview question is: "Tell me about yourself". Despite its apparent simplicity, this question can be challenging to answer. Let's start with what you shouldn't say.

Many of us fall into the trap of responding to this question by discussing their personal life or even recounting their life story. This is not what interviewers are looking for. Another common mistake interviewees make is citing unfavorable workplace issues as reasons for wanting to leave their current employment. Avoid making negative statements about current and former employers and colleagues.

Remember the elevator pitch? This is the perfect opportunity to use it. Focus on your skills and what you can do for the company. The interviewer wants to determine if you are a good fit for the position, so tailor your response to highlight your relevant experience and strengths.

Dressing appropriately and professionally is crucial, even for remote interviews. Ensure you look professional, and pay attention to your environment Choose a neutral background and check your audio and video settings prior the interview. Most importantly, practice your answers to common interview questions to ensure you come across as confident and prepared.

Some other questions are designed to assess your reactions in specific work situations, and this is where a particularly useful method comes in: the STAR method.

The STAR acronym stands for: Situation (giving context to your answer), Task (elaborating on the challenge and your role), Action (explaining how you can handle a particular situation), and Result (outcome or accomplishment).

Structuring your responses by this method is an effective way to prepare for possible questions in your interview. The Situation is where you set the stage for the story you are about to narrate by giving the interviewer some context pertaining to a particular situation or a challenge you have faced in the past. Keep your narration detailed but concise. The Task is where you give a description of your role or your responsibilities in relation to the situation or challenge initially described. The Action is where you explain what action you took including specific steps to solve the situation, and the Result is where you describe the outcome of your actions.

THE FOLLOW-UP

It is always good practice to send a brief thank you note the day after the interview. This sends a positive message to the interviewer and asserts your professionalism. It is also a chance for you to remind the hiring manager of your suitability for the role.

Note that part of the application and interview process involves a waiting period which can last for a few days or up to several weeks depending on the company's hiring process.

During the interview, it is best to inquire when you can expect feedback on your application, and interviewers would usually provide a timeframe for getting back to you. If you do not hear back within the timeframe provided, you may send a follow up email 1-2 days after the specified date, never earlier. An exception to this would be when there is an important and significant change to your portfolio that could positively affect the hiring decision, or if there are changes to your circumstances warranting your non-acceptance of any possible offer being made.

Register an entry in your calendar for sending a follow up mail. This mail should be written with a professional yet cordial tone, and include positive words about the company and/or your interview experience. As with the thank you note, the follow up mail should be concise and respectfully direct to the point.

You can always send a feedback note if you feel that the interview went well but your application was unsuccessful. Thank the interviewers for their time and ask them for feedback about your performance during the interview. As with the previous emails, use short, succinct sentences. The reality is, not every single interviewer will give you feedback, but it will be well worth a try.

NEGOTIATING SALARY AND CONTRACT TERMS

Begin researching the salary and contract terms of the position prior the interview stage, even if you are unsure about being hired. While ensuring you are likeable is essential to securing the job, it is equally important to understand the roles of the individuals you engage with. They may not only be hiring managers but also decision-makers regarding your salary. Always maintain professionalism and courtesy. Should there be an opportunity for you to negotiate salaries, be prepared for potential discussions and tension, and manage these situations with poise and professionalism.

If offered a salary lower than expected, articulate clearly why you deserve a higher amount. Touch on the value you bring to the company and your relevant experience. However, remain humble and realistic, recognizing that you are not irreplaceable, especially during the hiring process. Know your worth and advocate for appropriate compensation without overreaching. Avoid issuing ultimatums, as this can lead to the employer choosing another candidate over you.

To determine your position's worth, conduct thorough research to understand the typical earnings for individuals in similar roles with comparable experience. This information will support your compensation expectations.

During the interview, avoid discussing salary too early into the process. Instead, focus on the overall fit—how you can contribute to the company and in turn, how the company can support your career. Fixating on salary prematurely can raise concerns in the mind of the interviewer. When discussing salary, confidence is key. Have three figures in mind: an optimal, a reasonable, and a minimum acceptable salary. This approach will enable you to make informed decisions quickly.

After the interview, remember that you can ask questions and maintain honesty with both the interviewer and yourself. It is acceptable to decline the offer if the job does not align with your expectations or if the salary offered is significantly lower than anticipated.

MOCK INTERVIEW QUESTIONS

Let's explore some mock interview questions so you can better prepare for the interview. Keep in mind that these might not be the exact questions you will be asked but will most likely be similarly themed:

- What are the most critical skills for a VA?
- What attracted you to become a VA?
- How did you become a VA?
- What are your qualifications?
- What are your areas of expertise?
- What are your preferred tools to use as a VA?
- How would your co-workers describe you?
- Why do you want to work for this firm?
- What's your preferred work schedule?
- How many hours a week can you work?
- Do you have any questions for me?

KEY TAKEAWAYS

Chapter 8 explored strategies for excelling in interviews. Preparation is essential, and this includes researching the company's services, products, culture, values, and clientele. Knowledge about the interviewing company's business enhances your chances of getting hired.

During the interview, it is crucial to discuss both your hard and soft skills while demonstrating attributes such as organization, communication, time management, technical proficiency, and flexibility. Practicing your responses to common interview questions in advance is vital. Be ready to address inquiries about meeting deadlines, preferred tools, and handling multiple work assignments.

One frequently asked question that can be challenging to answer is, "Tell me about yourself." Avoid sharing personal details or discussing issues at your current job. Instead, deliver an elevator pitch focusing on your skills and how those can benefit the company.

Dress professionally for the interview, even if interviewed virtually. Use a neutral background and test your video and audio equipment beforehand to ensure everything functions correctly.

Send a thank you note the day after the interview. Ask questions on next steps during the interview. If you do not receive a response within the response timeline provided by the interviewer, send a follow-up message to express your continued interest in the position and offer to send any additional information they might need in support of your application.

If selected for the position, you will need to negotiate your salary and contract terms. Research industry salary ranges and justify your desired compensation by highlighting what you can offer the company with your skills and experience. Always have three salary figures in mind: an optimal amount, a reasonable amount, and a minimum acceptable amount.

FOLLOW-UP TEMPLATE

Dear (Name of the Interviewer),

I hope this email finds you well. I am writing to thank you for the opportunity to interview for the VA position with (Company Name).

After the interview, I became even more excited about potentially working at (Company Name). I value your perspective on the company's aims and challenges, which bolstered my conviction that with my experience and expertise, I would be a perfect match for the role.

Please feel free to get in touch with me should you require any additional information.

Thank you again for considering my application, and I look forward to the possibility of working together and helping in the success of (Company Name).

Regards,

(Your Name)

(Your Contact Information)

ITEMS TO BRING TO AN INTERVIEW & OTHER HELPFUL NOTES

- Multiple copies of your resume
- Your portfolio with samples of your work
- A list of professional references with their contact information

- A notepad and a pen to take notes during the interview
- Any form of identification
- Business cards (if you have had these printed)
- Prepare questions to ask about the company, the role, and how the team works.
- Dress professionally

CV/RESUME TEMPLATE

(Your Full Name in large letters)

(Your Address)

(Your City, State, and ZIP Code)

(Your Email Address)

(Your Phone Number)

(Your LinkedIn Profile URL)

Goal

Detail-oriented and organized VA with (number of years of experience) where I provided executive and administrative support. I have a proven track record of delivering high-quality outcomes in a fast-paced environment.

Professional Experience

Virtual Assistant (Company Name), (Location), (Month and Year)—present

- Perform various tasks to ensure the business runs smoothly.
- Provide remote and in-office administrative support.

- Manage schedules and coordinate meetings.
- Conduct research.

Administrative Assistant, (Previous Company), (Location), (Month and year of starting)—(Month and year of finishing)

- Provided remote administrative support.
- Provided remote executive support.
- Organized and maintained files, databases, and records
- Handled phone calls and emails

Skills

- Strong verbal and written communication skills
- Proficient in a variety of tools and platforms
- Proven ability to find solutions to problems
- Excellent organizational skills

Education

- (Degree earned, if any)
- (University Name, Location, and Date of Graduation)

Certification

- (Relevant Certification)

References

Available upon request.

TEMPLATE FOR INTERVIEW QUESTIONS

Interview Questions	Sample Answers	Your Answers
How did you get started as a VA?	After obtaining substantial administrative expertise in typical office settings, I switched to virtual support. Recognizing the trend toward remote work, I refined my abilities in digital tools and communication platforms, allowing me to seamlessly transition to virtual assistance.	
What drew you to become a VA?	The adaptability and potential for ongoing learning that come with becoming a VA drew me in. The opportunity to provide remote help to a variety of individuals and sectors meshes with my enthusiasm for offering complete administrative assistance.	
What are your preferred tools for working as a virtual assistant?	I am proficient in several tools, including (list of tools and platforms), which aid in effective communication, task management, and cooperation. My versatility enables me to swiftly become acquainted with new tools based on the role's unique requirements.	
What would your coworkers say about you?	Coworkers frequently characterize me as well-organized, dependable, and collaborative. I value straightforward communication and contribute positively to team dynamics, resulting in a cohesive and effective workplace.	

What makes you want to work for this company?	I feel inspired by (insert company's name)'s dedication to innovation and its reputation for investing in the development of its people. The match of my talents to the difficulties of the position excites me about contributing to the company's success.	
How many hours can you work every week?	I am adaptable and can commit to (insert number of hours you can work) hours per week, adapting as needed to meet project deadlines and successfully contribute to the success of the team.	

TEMPLATE FOR THE TELL ME ABOUT YOURSELF QUESTION

Questions (STAR Method)	Sample Answers	Your Answers
Situation	In my previous position as a VA, I worked on a pressing project for a client that required thorough coordination and effective task management. The objective was to provide high-quality solutions in a short period of time while incorporating various stakeholders and complicated elements of the project.	
Task	As the project's lead VA, my job was to arrange the project process, assign specific responsibilities to team members, and ensure that everyone communicated effectively. My responsibilities included managing priorities, controlling deadlines, and ensuring the quality of outputs.	
Action	To solve the issue, I created a thorough project management system that made use of technologies such as (insert tool or platform). I checked in with team members on a regular schedule to review progress, gave additional help as required, and enabled clear communication channels to remove any barriers as quickly as possible.	
Result	Our combined efforts not only met but even exceeded the client's expectations. We completed the job ahead of schedule while maintaining a high level of quality. This project's success confirmed my capacity to lead in difficult situations while ensuring the happiness of both clients and team members.	

TEMPLATE FOR A SALARY NEGOTIATION AND CONTRACT TERMS

VA's Salary Negotiation and Contract Terms	Sample Answer	Your Answer
Acknowledgment	I am grateful for extending the job of VA at (insert company's name). I welcome the opportunity and am looking forward to joining your team.	
Confirmation of Job Responsibilities	As we finalize the terms, I'd like to reiterate my essential duties as a VA to ensure everyone is on the same page.	
Discussion of Compensation	While I believe the proposed wage is competitive with the industry (if you do), I will want to discuss the potential of (insert any specific modifications or extra perks, if applicable) considering my expertise in (insert relevant experience).	
Inquiring About Benefits and Perks	Could we talk about the complete benefits package and any other advantages that come with the VA's position?	

CHAPTER NINE

YOU GOT THE JOB, NOW IT'S TIME TO SET UP YOUR HOME OFFICE

Your environment is the external hard drive where your habits are stored. This is to say that your surroundings and routines shape your habits and behaviors, and as a VA, your work environment shapes you. In this chapter, we will be looking at how you can set up your home office for maximum efficiency.

YOUR WORKSPACE

Having a dedicated space where you work is crucial to establishing boundaries and separating your work life from your personal life. This can be tricky when working from home. You should have an area in your home dedicated solely for your work space. Working on your kitchen or dining table is not ideal, as your brain associates that area and piece of furniture with eating and relaxation making it harder to focus.

Make sure your desk or home office is clean and always organized. When your workspace is tidy, you can better focus on what you are doing and increase your productivity. You must always be comfortable to prevent long-term health issues. Practice home office ergonomics: Use a chair that supports your spine and can be adjusted according to your height; ensure your monitor is positioned at or below eye level; ensure there is clearance for your knees, thighs, and feet under your desk; when typing keep your wrists straight and your arms closer to your body. You must also ensure that your workspace is well-lit, as dim lighting will make it harder for your eyes to focus, risking eye strain. Try to arrange for natural light in your workspace. Keep the area ventilated by opening doors and windows whenever possible.

Lastly, it is essential to minimize distractions to increase productivity while working. The best way to do this is to identify and remove potential causes of distraction, such as mobile phones, handheld gaming consoles, or any sources of loud or persistent noise.

HARDWARE

To work as a Virtual Assistant (VA), having the latest computer is not necessary unless your tasks require high-performance specifications. Generally, a reliable and well-functioning computer suffices. It is also advisable to have a backup device, such as a laptop, to ensure continuity in case your primary computer encounters issues.

A webcam is often necessary for video calls. While most laptops include built-in cameras, desktop users may need to purchase an external webcam. High-quality webcams with integrated microphones are relatively inexpensive. Additionally, noise-canceling headphones can enhance focus and productivity, although they are not always essential.

An external hard drive is recommended for backing up important documents, providing an extra layer of security against data loss due to computer failure or cyber attacks. Although many VAs use cloud services for data backup, having a physical backup is a prudent precaution.

Computer Specifications

When selecting a computer, consider your specific needs. General VA tasks do not require a high-end computer. The choice between a desktop and a laptop depends on your preference for mobility. Desktops are typically more affordable and easier to upgrade, whereas laptops offer portability.

For technical specifications, a computer with at least 8 GB of RAM, an Intel Core i5 processor (or AMD equivalent), and an SSD as the primary storage device is sufficient for most VA tasks. However, 16 GB of RAM and an Intel Core i7 processor (or AMD equivalent) are ideal for enhanced performance.

Software is another critical consideration. Essential tools include Slack, Google Workspace, Canva, Calendly, Hootsuite, Zoom, and Asana. These applications, covered in detail in Chapter 3, enhance productivity and facilitate efficient workflow management.

Security measures are paramount. Utilize password management tools to securely store and manage numerous passwords, ensuring they are strong and complex. Data security systems such as firewalls and antivirus software protect against malware and viruses, which is crucial given the volume of documents and emails you will handle. Cybersecurity applications, including VPNs, safeguard your communications and protect against unauthorized access.

By equipping yourself with the right hardware, software, and security measures, you can effectively perform your duties as a Virtual Assistant while maintaining data integrity and security.

INTERNET CONNECTIVITY

Your internet connectivity is crucial as it directly impacts your efficiency in online tasks. The absolute minimum required speed should be at least 3 Mbps, as some clients might not hire you without meeting this standard. However, having a download speed of 50 Mbps and an upload speed of 10 Mbps for optimal performance is ideal.

Even with a reliable internet connection, occasional outages may occur. These interruptions should not hinder your work. In such cases, your mobile data can be invaluable, as most computers and phones allow you to share mobile internet with your computer. Alternatively, consider having a prepaid broadband option as a backup.

DATA BACKUP

Data backup is essential for safeguarding your files and folders. You should not rely solely on your computer for storage. There are two primary options for data backup: cloud storage and physical storage. Ideally, you should utilize both.

Cloud storage is highly scalable, allowing you to purchase additional space as needed. It offers easy access from any location with internet connectivity, and automatic uploads ensure your data is consistently backed up. While cloud storage is generally secure, it is not immune to data breaches.

Physical storage, such as pen drives or hard drives, offers a faster backup and recovery solution that does not require an internet connection. These devices are portable and resistant to data breaches. However, they are susceptible to physical damage, which could result in data loss, and their scalability is limited.

For cloud backup, consider using reputable services such as Acronis, Paragon, or Carbonite. These options provide reliable solutions for safeguarding your data.

By ensuring robust internet connectivity and implementing effective data backup strategies, you can maintain productivity and protect your valuable information.

ACTION STEPS

Below is checklist of all the office essentials for your VA workspace:

- A desk
- A comfortable chair
- A laptop stand (if you have a laptop)
- A desk lamp
- Webcam (if needed)
- Headset
- Noise-canceling headphones
- Keyboard and mouse (if needed)

Having a functional home office will improve your productivity and make you feel more comfortable. It recommended to invest in quality equipment that ensures longevity and durability for long-term use. Quality office equipment is designed to endure usage over long periods without compromising performance or reliability, thus increasing your productivity.

In the following chapter, we will be talking about how you can find a balance between your work and your life, and we will talk about self-care as a VA.

KEY TAKEAWAYS

Now that you have secured the job, it is essential to create a dedicated workspace to help you focus on your duties. If you work from home, establish physical boundaries between your personal and professional life. Keep your workspace organized and clean to enhance productivity.

Invest in suitable hardware. A reliable computer is crucial, but it doesn't need to be extremely expensive—just adequate for your tasks. Additionally, consider having a backup computer, noise-canceling headphones, an external hard drive, and a webcam (if your computer doesn't have one). Internet connectivity is also vital; aim for a minimum of 3 Mbps, though higher speeds are preferable. Ensure you have a backup plan for internet outages, such as mobile data or prepaid broadband.

For data backup, use both cloud storage and physical storage. Cloud storage is scalable and easily accessible with an internet connection, while physical storage, like external hard drives, offers quick backup and recovery without needing internet access. Both methods provide security for your data.

Equip your home office with a desk, a comfortable chair, a desk lamp, a laptop stand (if needed), a keyboard and mouse, noise-canceling headphones, and a headset. Tailor these items to your specific tasks to create an efficient workspace.

CHAPTER TEN

WORK-LIFE BALANCE AND SELF-CARE AS A VA

B urnout doesn't demonstrate dedication to your job; it signifies neglect of your well-being. Maintaining a positive work-life balance is crucial, and the importance of adequate self-care cannot be overstated. In this chapter, we will explore various strategies for achieving a healthy work-life balance and promoting self-care. These techniques will help you prevent burnout and establish clear boundaries between your personal and professional life.

SETTING BOUNDARIES

Setting boundaries is crucial to separate your work life from your personal life, especially when working from home. Establish precise working hours to maintain a routine similar to an office environment, helping you manage work and avoid burnout. Communicate your limits to clients and coworkers by setting office hours and displaying them on social media profiles.

Learn to say no to manage your workload and prevent overcommitment. Use communication tools effectively, schedule breaks, and regularly assess your workload.

Family and Social Life Boundaries

Define a dedicated workspace and communicate your working hours to your family, ensuring they respect both. Discuss a schedule with your family to minimize distractions during work hours. Balance your time by scheduling quality moments with your family during breaks and after work.

For social interactions, be firm but polite when declining invitations during work hours. Inform your friends about your work schedule to avoid interruptions. Plan social activities in advance to maintain a healthy social life and practice self-care, ensuring a balanced lifestyle.

TIME MANAGEMENT

In this section, we're not going to cover time management as a tool, but about managing your time to maintain better work-life balance. The Pomodoro technique is highly effective for this purpose, helping you focus, reduce distractions, and increase productivity.

If you quickly get distracted throughout your workday, if you work way past the point of being productive, or if you have many open tasks but can't seem to finish them, then this technique will be helpful to you.

The Pomodoro Technique involves the following steps:

1. Choose a task.
2. Set a 25-minute timer.
3. Work exclusively on that task for 25 minutes.
4. Take a 5-minute break.
5. After four 25-minute sessions, take a 15-to-30-minute break.

Use a to-do list and a timer (such as your phone) to implement this technique. By breaking down complex projects into smaller tasks, you make them more manageable. Maintain discipline by avoiding distractions until the timer rings. Handle interruptions by taking your break early and restarting the Pomodoro.

Breaking down complex projects into smaller tasks makes it a lot easier to accomplish them. One task might take four Pomodoros, so you can break it down into four. But if you have a couple of tasks that take less than 25 minutes combined, you can do them in one Pomodoro. You must have discipline, and until the timer rings, you cannot get distracted by anything. No emails, no phones, no team chats—nothing. You will have time to go through them on your 5- or 30-minute break. Of course, there might be interruptions or incidents that you really must attend to. When this happens, you can take your 5-minute break and restart the Pomodoro.

PHYSICAL HEALTH

When you start working as a Virtual Assistant (VA), one of the most noticeable changes is adjusting to a home-based work environment, which may lead to a decline in physical activity. In an office setting, even without regular gym visits, the simple acts of commuting and interacting with coworkers contributes to your daily movement. Now, it's easy to fall into the routine of staying home for days, which can reduce your opportunities for physical activity and social interaction. This shift can negatively impact your work-life balance and overall health. So, what can you do to prevent becoming lethargic?

Simple Exercises

To counteract the sedentary nature of working from home, consider incorporating simple exercises into your daily routine. Start your day with a walk, replicating the movement you used to get from commuting. Take short walks during breaks, or choose to walk when running errands instead of driving. Investing in some basic gym equipment for your home, like a set of weights or an exercise ball, can also be beneficial. If you're unsure how to use them, there are plenty of online videos to guide you.

Yoga is another excellent option. It requires minimal equipment and can significantly improve your back and core strength, especially if you're sitting for extended periods. Regular stretching, even from your chair, can do wonders for your muscles and joints, helping to reduce muscle fatigue and improve blood circulation. For a more intense workout, consider exercises like burpees, lunges, and squats. These full-body exercises can be done anywhere and will help improve your posture and overall fitness. The challenge lies in creating a routine. Using techniques like the Pomodoro method, you can fit these exercises into your day and soon establish a healthy habit.

Nutrition

Maintaining a healthy diet is crucial for both physical and mental well-being, especially when working from home. Good nutrition keeps your energy levels high, enhancing focus and productivity. A diet lacking in essential nutrients can impair cognitive functions like problem-solving, focus, and memory. Poor nutrition can also lead to mood swings, increased stress, and a weakened immune system.

To eat healthily, start by drinking plenty of water to stay hydrated. Dehydration can significantly reduce concentration and cognitive function. Eat balanced meals throughout the day, incorporating a variety of vegetables, fruits, lean proteins, healthy fats, and whole grains. Choose healthy snacks like fruits, yogurt, nuts, and seeds, and avoid eating while working to maintain a clear division between meals and work time. Limit processed foods, caffeine, and sugar intake, as they can lower your energy levels. If necessary, consider nutritional supplements after consulting with a nutritionist.

Ergonomic Practices

A proper desk and chair setup is vital for ergonomic health in your home office. Your desk should be at a comfortable height, allowing your elbows to rest at a 90-degree angle close to your body. Your chair should be adjustable so that your feet are flat on the floor; if not, use a footrest. Ensure your chair provides lumbar support to maintain good posture. Wrist supports can also be beneficial while typing.

Other ergonomic considerations include using an external keyboard and mouse, positioning your monitor correctly, and ensuring good lighting. If your eyes tire quickly, consider using an anti-glare screen protector.

Other Considerations

To enhance your home office comfort and health, consider using fitness apps and trackers to stay motivated with your workouts. If you spend a lot of time alone, a pet can provide companionship and a reason to move daily. Activities like playing with a cat or walking a dog can improve both mental and cardiovascular health.

A standing desk is another excellent investment, allowing you to alternate between sitting and standing throughout the day, promoting movement and reducing the risks associated with prolonged sitting.

MENTAL HEALTH

While working from home offers flexibility, it's essential to maintain routines to protect your mental health. The stressors you face will differ from a traditional office setting, including balancing work and personal life and the pressure to always be available for clients. Self-care is crucial to mitigate these stresses. Prioritize your well-being through mindfulness and effective time management to avoid missed deadlines and excessive overtime.

Mindfulness

Mindfulness involves being present and aware of your thoughts and needs through techniques like yoga, breathing exercises, and meditation. It helps manage emotions and stress, contributing to overall mental well-being. Practices such as mindfulness-based cognitive therapy (MBCT) and mindfulness-based stress reduction (MBSR) can be particularly beneficial. MBCT combines mindfulness with cognitive behavioral therapy to prevent depression relapses, while MBSR focuses on reducing prolonged stress.

You can practice mindfulness individually or in a group, and many resources are available online. Simple techniques like mindful breathing, where you focus on your breath, and meditation, where you aim to clear your mind, can significantly enhance your mental health. Other forms of mindfulness include mindful walking and listening to music mindfully during daily activities.

CONTINUOUS LEARNING

As a VA, continuous learning is vital for staying competitive and avoiding burnout. Engaging in courses, workshops, and seminars, reading books, and attending networking events can enhance both your professional and personal skills. This ongoing development makes you more versatile and adaptable to various tasks and situations, improving your efficiency and employability.

Staying updated with technological advancements and industry trends is crucial. Familiarize yourself with new platforms, tools, and work processes to remain proficient and competitive. Participating in online courses, workshops, and webinars can provide hands-on experience and keep you informed about the latest industry developments.

Personal Development

Meeting and exceeding client expectations requires proficiency in the latest software, tools, and work methods. Exploring new platforms and tools, reading industry news, and taking online courses are effective ways to stay updated. Engaging in professional communities and seeking feedback from clients and colleagues can also provide valuable insights and opportunities for growth.

Develop a Growth Mindset

Cultivating a growth mindset helps you embrace challenges and view them as opportunities for growth. Being receptive to criticism, celebrating efforts regardless of the outcome, and seeking out challenging projects can foster continuous improvement. Encouraging this mindset in others promotes mutual support and collaboration.

Challenges and Setbacks

Don't just wait for challenges to find you; actively seek them beyond your comfort zone. You can do this by exploring projects and tasks that are unfamiliar to you so that you can expand your skill set. Embracing a growth mindset opens the door to such opportunities and enables you to foster this mindset in others, especially within long-term working relationships. Cultivating mutual support leads to better outcomes and efficiency.

Setbacks are inevitable, but they need not be viewed negatively. Like feedback and criticism, they serve as catalysts for growth. Use setbacks as learning opportunities by analyzing what went wrong and transforming them into actionable insights. Develop a personalized learning plan tailored to your unique strengths and weaknesses to facilitate growth and maintain focus on enhancing your capabilities. Visualization of success can be a powerful tool in reinforcing your growth mindset.

Be Flexible

Adaptability and flexibility are crucial for VAs working in dynamic environments. Being open to change, effectively managing your time, and maintaining transparent communication with clients and team members help you navigate uncertainties and meet evolving client needs.

Develop Problem-Solving Skills

Enhancing your problem-solving skills enables you to address challenges and adapt to different circumstances. Anticipating potential outcomes and planning for contingencies can help you prepare for disruptions, and mitigate any negative impact of unexpected shifts.

Seek Feedback

Seeking feedback is essential for self-awareness and continuous improvement. Actively solicit constructive feedback from both clients and colleagues to identify areas for growth and leverage your strengths. This fosters trust and enhances professional relationships, demonstrating your commitment to excellence.

Look Back on Your Day

Reflecting on your daily performance and keeping a journal can help you track progress, identify patterns, and make informed decisions for improvement. While initially challenging, consistent self-assessment enables meaningful growth. Reflect on the interactions you had with your clients throughout the day. Analyzing client interactions aids in assessing satisfaction and improving communication. Soliciting feedback from both clients and colleagues provides valuable perspectives and insights. Set performance goals based on feedback and self-reflection, focusing on areas for improvement.

Diversify Your Portfolio

Diversifying your client portfolio exposes you to various challenges, facilitating skill development. Learning from both successful and unsuccessful projects is crucial for growth. Taking on diverse and challenging projects cultivates problem-solving skills and enhances versatility. Showing proactive interest in such projects demonstrates readiness to step out of your comfort zone and expand your skill set.

Observe Goal-Setting

Setting goals is crucial for continuous learning. Goals provide direction and motivation, allowing for effective prioritization and progress measurement. Aligning personal goals with client objectives ensures contributions to project success. Regularly reviewing and adjusting goals ensures relevance and progress tracking. Recording progress provides valuable insights and fosters accountability. Aligning goals with client objectives underscores commitment to project success and client satisfaction.

By incorporating these practices into your daily routine, you can maintain physical and mental health, stay updated with industry trends, and continuously improve your skills as a VA.

ACTIONABLE STEPS AND PRACTICAL TIPS

This section outlines tips and actionable steps that will allow you to implement key points discussed in this chapter.

Have a Schedule

Balancing work as a virtual assistant (VA) with personal development starts with a well-structured schedule. Create a daily or weekly plan that allocates specific hours for work, relaxation, and personal growth. Following a consistent routine helps establish productive habits. Set clear priorities that support both professional and personal growth to better manage time and energy. Utilizing techniques like the Pomodoro method can further enhance focus and productivity by dividing the day into manageable intervals.

Set Goals

Setting realistic and achievable goals is crucial for maintaining a healthy work-life balance. Employ the SMART criteria (Specific, Measurable, Achievable, Relevant, Time-bound) to ensure goals are clear and attainable. Celebrating even small milestones boosts motivation and prevents burnout. Time management strategies, such as the Pomodoro technique, can be combined with mindfulness practices like meditation or yoga to reduce stress and enhance overall well-being.

Identify Priorities

Aligning priorities with overarching goals helps maintain focus on tasks that contribute most to success. Consider the long-term impact of tasks when setting priorities to avoid short-sighted decisions. Tools like the Eisenhower Matrix can aid in distinguishing between urgent and important tasks, ensuring critical tasks receive immediate attention. Regularly reviewing and adjusting priorities as circumstances change is essential for sustained progress.

Set Boundaries

Establishing clear boundaries between work and personal life is fundamental. A dedicated workspace, whether a home office or a designated corner, helps separate professional and personal activities. Define specific work hours and communicate these boundaries to friends, family, and clients. Clear communication ensures everyone understands when interruptions are acceptable and when they are not.

Politely Say No

Learning to decline additional tasks politely is vital to maintaining a balanced workload. When overwhelmed, it's important to refuse extra projects or tasks to protect your work-life balance. Declining unnecessary tasks prevents overcommitment and ensures you can focus on existing responsibilities effectively.

Be Proactive

Being proactive provides a competitive edge in the industry. Develop a personal development plan outlining steps toward achieving your goals. Regular self-assessment helps monitor progress, workload, and stress levels. Anticipate periods of increased workload and create strategies to manage them effectively, preventing feelings of overwhelm. Seek opportunities to develop skills through courses, workshops, or seminars to continuously advance your career.

Do Things That You Enjoy

Incorporate activities you enjoy into your daily routine to prevent burnout and enhance your work-life balance. Regularly evaluate and assess your priorities to ensure they remain aligned with your goals. Understand that balance is dynamic, requiring flexibility to adapt your schedule and activities according to changing circumstances. Being adaptable helps maintain a harmonious balance between work and personal life.

DAILY ROUTINE TEMPLATE

Day and time	Sample Activities/Food/Exercise for Body and Mind	Your Answers
Monday, 8:00 AM	Begin the day with a 15-minute stroll for physical activity. Make a nutritious breakfast that includes a variety of proteins, fruits, and whole grains. Check and prioritize the day's to-do list.	
Monday, 8:45 AM	Begin the first work session using the Pomodoro technique (25 minutes of intense work, followed by a 5-minute rest). During breaks, practice mindfulness breathing.	
Monday, 12:00 PM	Take a lunch break; avoid eating at your desk. Include veggies and lean meats and remain hydrated.	
Monday, 1:00 PM	Resume your job. Stretching exercises should be used during breaks to decrease muscular fatigue.	
Monday, 4:00 PM	Finish the workday with a final Pomodoro session. Review the finished work and make plans for the following day. Take a quick stroll to clear your head.	
Tuesday, 8:00 AM	Begin the day with a 15-minute stroll for physical activity. Make a nutritious breakfast that includes a variety of proteins, fruits, and whole grains. Check and prioritize the day's to-do list.	

Tuesday, 9:30 AM	Attend a personal development class or course online to improve your professional and personal abilities.	
Tuesday, 12:00 PM	Lunch break with a focus on a nutritious, well-balanced meal. Take a few moments to practice mindfulness meditation.	
Tuesday, 1:00 PM	Continue work. Incorporate yoga or stretches to maintain your physical well-being.	
Tuesday, 4:00 PM	Finish the workday with a final Pomodoro session. Review the finished work and make plans for the following day. Spend some quality time with your family.	
Wednesday, 8:00 AM	Begin the day with a 15-minute stroll for physical activity. Make a nutritious breakfast that includes a variety of proteins, fruits, and whole grains. Check and prioritize the day's to-do list.	
Wednesday, 9:00 AM	Join a networking event or connect with industry professionals.	
Wednesday, 12:00 PM	Lunch break with a balanced meal and hydration. Read a chapter of a personal development book.	
Wednesday, 1:00 PM	Return to work and incorporate quick exercises like lunges or squats between breaks.	

Wednesday, 4:00 PM	Finish the workday with a final Pomodoro session. Review the finished work and make plans for the following day. Prepare a well-balanced dinner.	
Thursday, 8:00 AM	Begin the day with a 15-minute stroll for physical activity. Make a nutritious breakfast that includes a variety of proteins, fruits, and whole grains. Check and prioritize the day's to-do list.	
Thursday, 8:45 AM	Participate in a mindfulness-based stress reduction session.	
Thursday, 12:00 PM	Lunch break with a focus on mindful eating and relation.	
Thursday, 1:00 PM	Return to work. Take breaks for stretching to improve posture.	
Thursday, 4:00 PM	Finish the workday with a final Pomodoro session. Review the finished work and make plans for the following day. Engage in a mindfulness meditation session before dinner.	
Friday, 8:00 AM	Begin the day with a 15-minute stroll for physical activity. Make a nutritious breakfast that includes a variety of proteins, fruits, and whole grains.	
Friday, 9:00 AM	Review the week's accomplishments and areas for improvement.	

Friday, 12:00 PM	Lunch break with a variety of vegetables and whole foods. Plan a self-care activity for the weekend.	
Friday, 1:00 PM	Complete client tasks and allocate time for continuous learning.	
Friday, 4:00 PM	Finish the workday with a final Pomodoro session. Review the finished work and send any necessary follow-up emails.	
Saturday and Sunday	Plan self-care activities such as reading, outdoors, meditation, etc.	

7-DAY GUIDE TO KICK-OFF AND SUSTAIN YOUR VA CAREER

Before concluding, here is a structured plan that can be integrated in the daily routine outlined in Chapter 10 to stay on course with your VA Career. Please note that these are recommendations, and you are encouraged to adapt them to your specific circumstances.

Day 1: Begin with the self-assessment provided in Chapters 1 and 2.

Day 2: Progress to the inventory steps as detailed in Chapters 3 and 4.

Day 3: Dedicate time to working on your portfolio template, following the instructions in Chapter 5.

Day 4: Focus on refining your elevator speech, cold outreach template, personal brand, and cover letter, as covered in Chapters 6 and 7.

Day 5: Delve into the chapters covering the follow-up template, resume enhancement, interview question template, crafting your "tell me about yourself" response, and strategies for salary negotiation.

Day 6: Take a moment to visualize your ideal workspace and compile a list of necessary items, as discussed in Chapter 9.

Day 7: Wrap up the week by prioritizing self-care and working on your self-care template from Chapter 10.

Print all the templates and store them in a binder or create a digital copy on your computer for easy access and updates as needed.

INSPIRE A NEW VA!

You've chosen a solid route to living a life with far greater freedom and flexibility than a traditional 9-5 could ever offer you, and that makes you the perfect person to inspire others to take the leap.

Simply by sharing your honest opinion of this book and a little about your own journey, you'll inspire new readers to start making the changes they've always wanted to make.

LET'S HEAR FROM YOU!
IF YOU ENJOYED THIS BOOK, PLEASE LEAVE A REVIEW TO HELP OTHERS

Thank you so much for your support, and I wish you the best of luck in all your endeavors.

"Scan the QR code below to leave your review on Amazon"

CONCLUSION

Starting a career as a VA holds immense promise and numerous opportunities today's world. When you have the right set of skills, the know-how to use practical tools, a positive attitude to learn, and a solid strategy can lead to a successful VA career. Being a VA offers not only financial success but also a balanced between professional and personal life. It provides the freedom to live more fully without being tied to a 9-to-5 job or stuck in the same office for years.

In summary, remember **R.E.M.O.T.E.** The Blueprint for VA Success!

Research market needs where your services are in high demand.

Evaluate your skills against those needs and find ways to align them.

Master the tools to complement your skills and match those market needs.

Optimize your portfolio to increase your chances of getting noticed in the competitive VA job market.

Tackle interviews with confidence and skills to maximize your chances of getting hired.

Establish work-life balance as a high-value, high-performance VA, ensuring long-term sustainability and preventing burnout.

REFERENCES

Academy, R. (2023, March 17). *Handling stress as a virtual assistant: Success tips*. Rozi Academy. https://www.roziacademy.com/coping-with-stress-as-a-virtual-assistant-strategies-for-success-are-you-tired-of-the-daily-grind

Birt, J. (2019). *How to use the STAR interview response technique*. Indeed. https://www.indeed.com/career-advice/interviewing/how-to-use-the-star-interview-response-technique

Bottleneck Distant Assistants. (2017, January 27). *Identifying virtual assistants: General VA vs specialized VA*. QuickBookshttps://bottleneck.online/identifying-virtual-assistants-general-va-vs-specialized-va/

Bottorff, S., & Bottorff, C. (2023, January 2). *What is QuickBooks & how does it work?* Forbes. https://www.forbes.com/advisor/business/software/what-is-quick books/#:-

Clockify content team. (2023, June 5). *Setting up a new Clockify workspace*. Clockify Learn. https://clockify.me/learn/resources/setting-up-new-account/

Friday App content team. (n.d.). *Slack overview: An introduction & answers to your questions*. FridayApp. https://friday.app/p/slack-overview

Gardner, B. (2017, September 20). *Get more virtual assistant clients: How to write a cold pitch email*. Desire to Done. https://desiretodone.com/how-to-write-a-cold-pitch-email/

Grand View Research. (2018). *Intelligent virtual assistant market size | IVA industry report, 2018-2024*Forbes. https://www.grandviewresearch.com/industry-analysis/intelligent-virtual-assistant-industry

He, G. (2022, September 15). *17 top virtual assistant skills to get hired in 2023*. Teambuilding. https://teambuilding.com/blog/virtual-assistant-skills

Hoory, L., & Leonard, K. (2023, September 15). *FreshBooks review: Google Drive*. Forbes. https://www.forbes.com/advisor/business/software/freshbooks-review/

Kriss, R., & Crawford, H. (2023, June 30). *Wave accounting review: Pros, cons, alternatives*. NerdWallet. https://www.nerdwallet.com/article/small-business/wave-accounting-review

Le, Rachel. "50+ Inspiring Quotes on Remote Work to Keep You Motivated." Esevel. Last modified November 13, 2023. https://esevel.com/blog/quote-of-remote-work.

MacKenzie, K. (2023, July 18). *The HR virtual assistant boom: A deep dive into the surge*. Recruiting Resources: How to Recruit and Hire Better. https://resources.work able.com/stories-and-insights/hr-virtual-assistant#:-

Markets, R. and. (2023, August 18). *Healthcare virtual assistants: Global market analysis and business strategies report 2023-2030 - chatbots anticipated to experience massive growth.* GlobeNewswire News Room. https://www.globenewswire.com/news-release/2023/08/18/2727842/28124/en/Healthcare-Virtual-Assistants-Global-Market-Analysis-and-Business-Strategies-Report-2023-2030-Chatbots-Antici pated-to-Experience-Massive-Growth.html

Nath, B. (2022, March 15). *Cloud backup vs. local backup: Which is better?* Geekflare. https://geekflare.com/cloud-backup-vs-local-backup/

Nicholls, L. (2023, April 10). *The best online job sites for virtual assistants in 2022.* Fully Booked VA. https://fullybookedva.com/how-find-virtual-assistant-jobs/

No Blue content team. (2015, February 16). *Top 10 Google Drive features: Business management solutions.* NoBlue. https://noblue.co.uk/news-updates/b2b/top-ten-google-drive-features/

Obligana-Pango, M. (n.d.). *How do you choose the right projects and samples to include in your virtual assistant portfolio?* LinkedIn. https://www.linkedin.com/advice/1/how-do-you-choose-right-projects-samples-include

Online job hunters content team. (2023, July 16). *How to secure your first client as a free-lancer or virtual assistant.* https://onlinejobhunters.com/how-to-secure-your-first-client-as-a-freelancer-or-virtual-assistant/

Payscale Team. (n.d.). *Virtual assistant hourly pay in 2023.* Payscale. https://www.payscale.com/research/US/Job=Virtual_Assistant/Hourly_Rate

RescueTime content team. (n.d.). *Getting started with rescuetime.* Newrescuetime. https://newrescuetime.helpscoutdocs.com/article/294-getting-started-with-rescue time-premium

Rose. (2021, October 14). *How to create your virtual assistant portfolio when you have little or no experience Pomodoro.* The Rosepreneur. https://therosepreneur.com/virtual-assistant-portfolio/

Scroggs, L. (2022). *The Pomodoro technique – why it works & how to do it.* Todoist. https://todoist.com/productivity-methods/pomodoro-technique

Smart Virtual Assistants Content Team. (n.d.). *Must-Have virtual assistant hard skills and soft skills.* Smart VAs. https://smartvirtualassistants.com/blog/must-have-virtual-assistant-hard-skills-and-soft-skills

Tibon, B. (2020, February 10). *The increasing demand for virtual assistants in 2022.* My Cloud Crew. https://mycloudcrew.com/the-increasing-demand-for-virtual-assis tants/

Uassist.ME Team. (2020, August 7). *A brief history of virtual assistants.* Uassistme. https://www.uassistme.com/blog/a-brief-history-of-virtual-assistants

UNT content team. (n.d.). *One drive for business and office 365 | college of health and public service.* HPS. https://hps.unt.edu/it/one-drive-business-and-office-365

We Are Indy Content Team. (2022, December 27). *How much do virtual assistants make?* Indy. https://weareindy.com/blog/how-much-do-virtual-assistants-make